ILLUSTRATED BY BILL TIDY

The
Bedside Book
of Final Words

COMPILED BY ERIC GROUNDS

Introduced by Richard Stilgoe

AMBERLEY

First published 2014

Amberley Publishing
The Hill, Stroud
Gloucestershire, GL5 4EP

www.amberley-books.com

British Library Cataloguing in Publication Data.
A catalogue record for this book is available from the British Library.

ISBN 978 1 4456 4453 0 (paperback)
ISBN 978 1 4456 4464 6 (ebook)

Typeset in 10pt on 12pt Minion Pro.
Typesetting and Origination by Amberley Publishing.
Printed in the UK.

Contents

Introduction
by Sir Richard Stilgoe

As if being christened Eric wasn't tough enough, Eric Grounds has bravely faced a lifetime of challenges. He has raised millions for national charities, been High Sheriff of Northumberland and best man at a royal wedding. In the course of all this he will have had to address many public gatherings. Addressing public gatherings – which, after a bit of practice, can become quite addictive – gives you an opportunity to do small and inaccurate pieces of market research; you can ask the audience questions like, 'How many of you in this room have ever stolen something from a shop?' Usually about 5 per cent of hands go up. Then you ask the audience to shut their eyes, and when they all have their eyes closed you ask the same question again, and this time about 30 per cent of them put up their hands. Which is interesting, but not as interesting as the next question. 'Right,' you say. 'How many people in this room are going to die?' There is a nervous titter, and gradually fewer than half the people in the room raise their hands. Honestly – try it.

We Brits are more in denial about death than any other subject, so any attempt to lighten the subject up a bit is especially welcome, and this useful book will do just that. Spike Milligan wanted to go on making people smile after he died, so directed that his gravestone should bear the words, 'I told you I was ill.' This caused no end of a fuss, with the church getting involved, and produced a very British compromise; Spike was mostly Irish, so his headstone in Winchelsea in Sussex bears the words, 'Duirt me leat go raibh me breoite,' which is Gaelic for – you guessed it – 'I told you I was ill.'

The tricky thing in the last words business, as in so much else, is timing. Do you think of something clever years before and try and remember it to trot out at the appropriate time? Do you rely on last-minute inspiration? How can you control your last seconds so that you say your pithy sentence, check that someone's got it down accurately, then die? What if you say it, then feel better? You might have to keep quiet for hours before you finally snuff it. Imagine Pitt the Younger saying, 'I think I could eat one of Bellamy's veal pies,' then perking up a bit, and somebody fetching him one, and Pitt the Younger saying, 'Thanks – that really hit the spot!' and then going. He wouldn't have made it into the book.

On the timing thing, my favourite in the whole book is the one where the timing is *nearly* right. General John Sedgwick, in the heat of an American battle in 1864, dismissed the enemy's shooting skills with the words, 'They couldn't hit an elephant at this dist– '

I am going to follow his example. When the time comes, surrounded by my large and loving family, I shall say, 'I have been saving up for years, and I have left each of you a million pounds. It is buried in the– '

All of us would like to have that much control at the end. Heaven preserve us from situations where our last words are, 'Why did we have to come all the way to Switzerland?'

Richard Stilgoe

Limpsfield, 2014

Artists, Musicians, Poets and Writers

Joseph Addison, 1672–1719
'See in what peace a Christian can die.'

Founder of *The Spectator* with his long-standing friend Richard Steele, who had already established *Tatler*.

He served as Secretary of State for the Southern Department from 1717 to 1718 and produced a slightly zany government newspaper, *The Freeholder*, which most people criticised. Alexander Pope called him 'Atticus' in an effort to diminish him. He fell out with Steele over the Peerage Bill of 1719. He was forced to resign as Secretary of State in 1718 because of his poor health, but remained an MP until his death at Holland House, London, on 17 June 1719, aged forty-seven. He is buried in Westminster Abbey.

His final words were, 'See in what peace a Christian can die.'

Louisa May Alcott, 1832–1888
'Is it not meningitis?'

American novelist known for her book *Little Women*. She experienced health problems for many years and both she and her early biographers attributed this to her treatment with a mercury compound used to counter typhoid during the American Civil War. Later analysis suggested that she had problems with her auto-immune system and it has been suggested that she had lupus. She died having had a stroke two days after the death of her father. Her last words were, 'Is it not meningitis?'

François-Marie Arouet (see Voltaire)

Jane Austen, 1775–1817
'Nothing but death ... '

The English novelist who wrote romantic fiction characterised by sharp irony. Well-known works include *Pride and Prejudice*, *Northanger Abbey*, *Sense and Sensibility*, and *Mansfield Park*.

From 1816 her health declined steadily until it was apparent to all that she was very sick. In 1964 Dr. Vincent Cope suggested that she had Addison's disease. Others described her final illness as Hodgkin's lymphoma. Katherine White of Britain's Addison's Disease Self Help Group suggests that Austen probably died of bovine tuberculosis, a disease associated with drinking unpasteurized milk.

When asked by her sister, Cassandra, if there was anything she wanted, she replied, 'Nothing but death.' Her final written words were, 'Rather longer petticoats than last year ... '

Sir James M. Barrie, 1860–1937
'I can't sleep.'

The Scottish author who invented Peter Pan. He was created a Baronet in 1913 and was awarded the Order of Merit in 1922. He gave the rights to the Peter Pan stories to London's Great Ormond Street Hospital, which continues to benefit from them. He died of pneumonia on 19 June 1937, having said, 'I can't sleep.'

L. Frank Baum, 1856–1919
'Now we can cross the shifting sands.'

The American author of children's books who wrote *The Wonderful Wizard of Oz*. On 5 May 1919, Baum had a stroke. He died quietly the next day, nine days short of his sixty-third birthday. At the end he mumbled in his sleep, then said, 'Now we can cross the shifting sands.'

Aubrey Beardsley, 1872–1898
'I am imploring you – burn all the indecent poems and drawings.'

English illustrator and author who died at the age of twenty-five from tuberculosis in the Cosmopolitan Hotel in Menton, France. His final words were 'I am imploring you – burn all the indecent poems and drawings.'

Ludwig van Beethoven, 1770–1827
'Ich werde im Himmel hören!' or 'Schade, schade, zu spät.'

Probably one of the most influential composers of all time. He was almost entirely deaf during the last decade of his life.

He died during a thunderstorm on 26 March 1827. There are three versions of his last recorded words: 'Ich werde im Himmel hören!' ('I shall hear in Heaven!') and 'Plaudite, amici. Comedia finita est' ('Friends, applaud. The comedy is finished.'). This was the traditional conclusion to performances of Italian commedia dell'arte and Anselm Huttenbrenner, who was present at the death in company with Beethoven's sister-in-law, specifically denied that he had said the words on his deathbed.

The third version is that he was told that he had been sent twelve bottles of wine by his publisher. His response was, 'Schade, schade, zu spät.' ('Pity, pity – too late.')

Arnold Bennett, 1867–1931
'Everything's gone wrong, my girl.'

English novelist and journalist. He won a literary competition managed by *Tit-Bits* magazine in 1889. This persuaded him to become a journalist. In 1894, he became assistant editor of the periodical *Woman*. His first novel, *A Man from the North*, was well received. From 1900 he became a full-time writer. His non-fiction work has endured and one of the most popular is the self-help book *How to Live on 24 Hours a Day*.

He died of typhoid in his Baker Street home in London. His final words to his mistress, Dorothy Cheston, were said to be, 'Everything's gone wrong, my girl.'

Sir Isaiah Berlin, 1909–1997
'And where do you come from?'

British of Russian-Jewish origin, he was a social and political thinker, philosopher and historian. Some commentators claim that he was the dominant scholar of his generation. He was a top-class conversationalist and raconteur and was renowned for his skills as a lecturer. He died in Oxford and his final words were reported by his nurse, who was asked, 'And where do you come from?'

Johannes Brahms, 1833–1897
'Ah, der schmeckt schön. Danke.'

A leading composer and musician of the Romantic period. He died of cancer on 3 April 1897. He was extremely thirsty and was given a glass of wine. His last words were reported to be 'Ah, der schmeckt schön. Danke.' ('Ah, that tastes nice. Thank you.')

Anne Brontë, 1820–1849
'Take courage, Charlotte, take courage.'

The youngest member of the Brontë family, she died of consumption while staying in Scarborough. On 28 May 1849, in the company of her sister Charlotte and Charlotte's great friend Ellen Nussey, she said, 'Take courage, Charlotte, take courage.'

Charlotte Brontë, 1816–1855
'He will not separate us. We have been so happy.'

English novelist and poet, the eldest of three surviving daughters of Patrick and Maria Brontë of Thornton in Yorkshire. Her famous novel, *Jane Eyre*, was written under the pen name Currer Bell. She eventually agreed to marry Arthur Bell Nicholls, her father's curate, who had loved her for some time. They wed in June 1854.

She died with her unborn child on 31 March 1855, possibly from typhus, although there has been much debate about the assorted ailments that caused her early death. The death certificate gives the cause of death as phthisis (tuberculosis). Her final words to her husband were, 'Oh, I am not going to die, am I? He will not separate us. We have been so happy.'

Elizabeth Barrett Browning, 1806–1861
'Beautiful.'

The prominent Victorian poet. In reply to her husband's question about how she felt, she responded, 'Beautiful,' and then died on 29 June 1861.

Michelangelo Buonarotti, 1475–1564
'Ancora imparo.'

Italian sculptor, painter, architect, poet and engineer who was a driving force in the development of Western art. Among his most famous works are the ceiling of the Sistine Chapel, the *Pietà* in the Vatican and *David*. He wrote over three hundred sonnets and madrigals. Dying naturally as an old man, he is reported to have said, 'Ancora imparo.' ('I'm still learning.')

Robert Burns, 1759–1796
'Don't let the awkward squad fire over me.'

Known as the Ploughman Poet, the Bard of Ayrshire or, more generally, the Bard. He was an early man of the Romantic movement. He experienced poor health and is thought to have had a rheumatic heart condition which, according to the temperance activist James Currie, was exacerbated by drink. Whether they were his final words or not is open to debate, but it is commonly accepted that he said, 'Don't let the awkward squad fire over me.'

Lord George Byron, 1788–1824
'I leave something dear to the World.'

English poet and leading figure of the Romantic movement. His life was one of great excess, notably with debts and love affairs. He fell ill in February 1824 and was further weakened by the common practice of bloodletting. He died on 19 April, possibly from sepsis caused by unsterilised medical equipment. He is supposed to have called out place names and numbers, then the names of those he loved and then 'Io lascio qualque cosa di caro nel mondo.' ('I leave something dear to the World.')

Another version is, 'Now I shall go to sleep. Goodnight.'

Thomas Carlyle, 1795–1881
'So this is death ... well ... '

Scottish essayist, historian and philosopher. He spent a number of years as Rector of Edinburgh University, but spent his latter days in London, living in Cheyne Row. It was suggested that he might be buried in Westminster Abbey, but he had specifically asked to be buried beside his parents in Ecclefechan cemetery. His last words are said to have been, 'So this is death ... well ... '

Nicolas-Sebastian Chamfort, 1741–1794
'Ah! mon ami, je m'en vais enfin de ce monde, où il faut que le cœur se brise ou se bronze.'

French writer who is remembered for his epigrams and aphorisms. He was secretary to the cousin of Louis XVI.

He was briefly imprisoned in 1793 but was released. He discovered that he was about to be arrested again and, determined not to let it happen a second time, in September 1793 he locked himself in his office and shot himself in the face. He hit his nose and part of his jaw but didn't die, so he stabbed his neck with a paper cutter, failing to cause terminal damage. Finally he used the paper cutter to stab himself in the chest. He dictated a final declaration, 'Moi, Sebastien-Roch Nicolas de Chamfort, déclare mon désir de mourir en homme libre plutôt que d'être reconduit en esclave dans une maison d'arrêt,' ('I, Sebastien-Roch Nicolas de Chamfort, hereby declare my wish to die a free man rather than to continue to live as a slave in a prison.') and signed it in a firm hand with his own blood. His butler later found him unconscious. From then until his death in Paris the following year, he suffered intensely and was attended to by a gendarme, whom he paid a crown a day.

He did not die until 13 April 1794 and nobody has recorded any words that he may have spoken. But the Abbe Sieyes did record a bon mot which has become the accepted version of his final words: 'Ah! mon ami, je m'en vais enfin de ce monde, où il faut que le cœur se brise ou se bronze.' ('Ah, my friend, I leave this world at last, where the heart must break or bronze.')

Anton Pavlovich Chekhov, 1860–1904
'Это давно я не пил шампанского.'

Russian physician, dramatist and author. He practised medicine throughout his life while nurturing his writing. He is reported to have said, 'Medicine is my lawful wife and literature is my mistress.'

On his deathbed with terminal tuberculosis, he sat up and said loudly, 'Ich sterbe.' ('I'm dying.') The doctor gave him an injection of camphor, and ordered champagne. Chekhov took a glass, examined it, smiled at Olga, his wife, and said, 'Это давно я не пил шампанского.' ('It's a long time since I drank champagne.') He drained it, lay quietly on his left side, and died.

Frederic Chopin, 1810–1849
'Jouez Mozart en mémoire de moi et je vais vous entendre.'

The prolific Polish composer and pianist who is commonly regarded as one of the great masters of Romantic music. In September 1849, he took a large apartment in the Place Vendôme (paid for by one of his wealthy pupils, Jane Stirling). Over the course of the next month, his health deteriorated, possibly because of tuberculosis. During the two days before he died, he asked for a piece of paper and wrote, 'Comme cette terre m'étouffera, je vous conjure de faire ouvrir mon corps pour (que)'je ne sois pas enterré vif.' ('As this earth will suffocate me, I implore you to have my body opened so that I will not be buried alive.')

In the event, these were not his last words. Shortly after midnight on 17 October his physician asked him if he was suffering greatly. Chopin whispered, 'Pas encore.' ('No longer.') He died shortly afterwards. Some sources say that his very last words were, 'Jouez Mozart en mémoire de moi et je vais vous entendre.' ('Play Mozart in memory of me – and I will hear you.')

Paul Claudel, 1868–1955
'Docteur, pensez-vous que cela aurait pu être la saucisse?'

French poet and dramatist who was a career diplomat, serving as ambassador in Tokyo, Washington and Brussels. He was not an easy man. His devout Catholicism and right-wing views made him unpopular. He died in Paris and there is no particular reason for his last words to have been recorded, but the theory is that he said, 'Docteur, pensez-vous que cela aurait pu être la saucisse?' ('Doctor, do you think it could have been the sausage?')

Kurt Cobain, 1967–1994
'I love you. I love you.'

American singer-songwriter who was the lead singer and guitarist of Nirvana. He struggled with heroin addiction, depression and illness.

The suicide note found with his body several days after he shot himself said, 'I have not felt the excitement of listening to as well as creating music, along with really writing ... for too many years now.' It went on to say, 'Frances and Courtney, I'll be at your altar. Please keep going Courtney, for Frances for her life will be so much happier without me. I LOVE YOU. I LOVE YOU.'

Samuel Taylor Coleridge, 1772–1834
'My mind is quite unclouded. I could even be witty.'

English poet, critic and philosopher who was a friend of Wordsworth and a founder member of the Lake Poets. Throughout his life he experienced bouts of depression and illness, which contributed to a serious addiction to opium. His ailments alienated him from his family so he spent the last eighteen years of his life living in the home of his physician, James Gillman, in Highgate. Gillman is credited with controlling the opium addiction.

His last words were, 'My mind is quite unclouded. I could even be witty.'

His epitaph is, 'Beneath this sod; A Poet lies; or that which once was he; O lift one thought in prayer for S.T.C.; That he, who many a year with toil of breath; Found Death in Life, may here find Life in Death.'

Noel Coward, 1899–1973
'Good night my darlings. I'll see you tomorrow.'

English playwright, composer, director, actor and singer, the son of a piano salesman. His nickname, 'The Master', 'started as a joke and became true', according to Coward. It was used of him from the 1920s onwards and he used it to cultivate his own style. He died of heart failure at his home in Jamaica on 26 March 1973. On retiring to bed the night before, he said, 'Good night my darlings. I'll see you tomorrow.'

Hart Crane, 1899–1932
'Goodbye everybody.'

An American poet who committed suicide at the age of thirty-two by jumping off the cruise ship SS *Orizabal* in the Gulf of Mexico. His behaviour was affected by some years of depression and elation, largely mixed with or by alcohol and shortly before his death he was severely beaten after making sexual advances towards a male crew member. His parting words were, 'Goodbye, everybody!' His body was never found.

Salvador Dali, 1904–1989
'¿Dónde está mi reloj?'

Spanish surrealist painter born in Figueres, Spain. His eccentric manner and attention-grabbing public actions sometimes drew more attention than his artwork and he used this consciously to promote himself.

On 23 January 1989, while listening to his favourite recording of *Tristan and Isolde*, he died of heart failure at Figueres at the age of eighty-four.

His last words were supposed to have been, '¿Dónde está mi reloj?' ('Where is my clock?')

Walter de la Mare, OM, CH, 1873–1956
'Too late for fruit. Too soon for flowers.'

English poet and novelist who wrote about 100 stories, of which 40 per cent were ghost stories. He had a coronary thrombosis in 1947 and died of another in 1956. His ashes are buried in the crypt of St Paul's Cathedral where he had once been a choirboy.

His final words are often quoted as, 'Too late for fruit. Too soon for flowers,' but there is no evidence that they were, in fact, the last words he spoke.

Charles Dickens, 1812–1870
'Yes. On the ground.'

English author and social critic. During the last two years of his life he undertook a national tour of 'farewell readings'. His health was failing and he often felt giddy, occasionally accompanied by paralysis. He collapsed on 22 April 1869, at Preston in Lancashire. On the instruction of his doctor, the remainder of the tour was cancelled. He did undertake a limited attempt to complete the tour but on 8 June 1870, he suffered another stroke at his home, after a full day's work on *Edwin Drood*. He never regained consciousness and died at Gad's Hill Place.

Someone had said to him in his final moments that he ought to lie down and his final words were, 'Yes, on the ground.'

Emily Dickinson, 1830–1886
'I must go in. The fog is rising.'

American poet. She died of Bright's disease (a form of kidney disease), which lasted for two and a half years. She was confined to her bed for several

* DUNNO, MATE! IT SEZ HERE...
DE LA MARE, THE CRYPT, WESTMINSTER ABBEY!'.

months before her death, so it is hard to interpret her alleged final words – 'I must go in. The fog is rising.' She was offered a glass of water and responded, 'Oh, is that all it is?'

Willie Donaldson, 1935–2005
'You're a lifesaver, Andy.'

Son of a shipping magnate, old Wykehamist, writer (he was the author of the Henry Root letters), satirist and founder of *Beyond the Fringe*, who spent three fortunes through adventurous living and generosity. The caretaker of his building collected some pills for Donaldson, prompting him to utter his final words, 'You're a lifesaver, Andy.' The source is Terence Blacker's excellent biography, *You Cannot Live as I Have and Not End Up Like This*.

Mary Ann Evans, better known as George Eliot, 1819–1880
'Tell them I have a great pain in my left side.'

English novelist, journalist and translator, the author of *Middlemarch*. She adopted a male pen name in order to ensure that her works were treated seriously. For twenty years she lived with a married man, George Henry Lewes, who had a legitimate wife, Agnes Jervis. Agnes was content with her husband's behaviour because she lived with Thornton Leigh Hunt and had four children with him. Lewes died in November 1878 and eighteen months later, Mary Ann married John Cross, a man twenty years younger than herself.

Their honeymoon was disrupted when John Cross either fell or jumped from their balcony into the Grand Canal in Venice. He survived and they returned to England but Mary Ann came down with a throat infection. This, coupled with the kidney disease she had been afflicted with for the previous few years, led to her death on 22 December 1880 at the age of sixty-one. It is said that she had just been given the highly unsuitable treatment of cold beef jelly and an egg whipped up in brandy, so her final words were, 'Tell them I have great pain in my left side.'

Ian Fleming, 1908–1964
'I am sorry to trouble you chaps. I don't know how you get along so fast with the traffic on the roads these days.'

English author and journalist who had been a naval intelligence officer during the Second Word War. He is best known for his *James Bond* spy novels. Fleming came from a wealthy family connected to the merchant bank Robert Fleming & Co.

On 11 August 1964, Fleming walked to the Royal St George's Golf Club for lunch and later dined with friends at his hotel in Canterbury. He collapsed with a heart attack shortly after he had eaten. He died in the early morning of 12 August 1964. His last recorded words were an apology to the ambulance drivers, saying, 'I am sorry to trouble you chaps. I don't know how you get along so fast with the traffic on the roads these days.'

Bernard de Fontenelle, 1657–1757
'Je ne ressens rien, à part une certaine difficulté à continuer à exister.'

He trained in the law but gave up after one case in order to devote his life to writing about philosophers and scientists. He was popular and held in great esteem. Unlike Voltaire, Fontenelle avoided making important enemies. He always balanced his criticism with flattery and praise.

He attributed his longevity to eating strawberries and he remained highly vigorous until the end of his life. One woman wrote of him at the age of ninety-two that he was as lively as a man of twenty-two. In his late nineties he met the beautiful Madame Helvétius and allegedly said to her, 'Ah Madame, if only I were eighty again!'

Fontenelle's last words are generally reported as, 'Je ne ressens rien, à part une certaine difficulté à continuer à exister.' ('I feel nothing, apart from a certain difficulty in continuing to exist.') The trouble is that there is no evidence to support this.

Benjamin Franklin, 1706–1790
'A dying man can do nothing easy.'

One of the founding fathers of the United States, he was a celebrated polymath: scientist, author, political theorist, musician, inventor, satirist, civic activist, statesman and diplomat. Among his inventions were the lightning rod, bifocal glasses and a flexible urinary catheter.

His death is described in detail in the book *The Life of Benjamin Franklin*. An abcess had formed in his lungs. When it burst, he threw up great quantities of fluid. Eventually he was overwhelmed by lethargy and on 17 April 1790, at about 11 p.m., he quietly died.

The account of his death gives some substance to his apparent final words. His daughter asked him to change position to improve his breathing and he said, 'A dying man can do nothing easy.'

Thomas Gainsborough, 1727–1788
'We are all going to Heaven, and van Dyke is of the company.'

English portrait and landscape painter, the son of a Suffolk weaver, who died of cancer at the age of sixty-one. His final words were, 'We are all going to Heaven, and van Dyke is of the company.'

Marvin Gaye, 1939–1984
'Mother, I'm going to get my things and get out of this house. Father hates me and I'm never coming back.'

The American singer-songwriter with a series of top-selling albums. On 1 April 1984 he was at his parents' house and had a violent argument with his father. He said, 'Mother, I'm going to get my things and get out of this house. Father hates me and I'm never coming back.' Moments later he was shot dead by his father, Marvin Gaye Snr.

Sir William Gilbert, 1836–1911
'Put your hands on my shoulders and don't struggle.'

English dramatist and librettist. He produced fourteen comic operas in collaboration with the composer Sir Arthur Sullivan.

He was not an easy man, but he absolutely loved children. On 29 May 1911, he was giving a swimming lesson to two girls, Winifred Isabel Emery (1890–1972) and seventeen-year-old Ruby Preece, in the lake of his home, Grim's Dyke, when Preece lost her footing and called for help. Gilbert dived in to save her and said, 'Put your hands on my shoulders and don't struggle.' He then had a heart attack and died.

Charlotte Perkins Gilman, 1860–1935
'It is the simplest of human rights to choose a quick and easy death in place of a slow and horrible one.'

American sociologist, novelist and lecturer for social reform. She was inclined to depression, which was not improved by marriage and motherhood. Many of her diary entries from the time she gave birth to her daughter described the symptoms of depression. In her suicide note she wrote, 'When all usefulness is over, when one is assured of an unavoidable and imminent death, it is the simplest of human rights to choose a quick and easy death in place of a slow and horrible one.'

Johann Wolfgang von Goethe, 1749–1832
'Komm, meine Kleine, und gib mir deine Hand.'

German writer, artist and politician who was a literary celebrity by the age of twenty-five. He died in Weimar in 1832 and there are two versions of his last words. The first is 'Mehr Licht' ('More light'), apparently as an instruction to a servant to open a shutter to let in more of the morning sun. The second, allegedly to his daughter-in-law Ottilie von Pogwisch, who cared for him during his latter years, was, 'Komm, meine Kleine, und gib mir deine Hand.' ('Come, my little one, and give me your hand.')

Joseph Haydn, 1732–1809
'Meine Kinder, keine Angst zu haben, den wo Haydn ist, kann nicht Schaden fallen.'

Austrian composer who is often called the 'Father of the Symphony' and 'Father of the String Quartet'.

He died, aged seventy-seven, at the end of May 1809, shortly after an attack on Vienna by the French army under Napoleon. Among his last words was his attempt to calm and reassure his servants when cannon shot fell in the neighbourhood: 'Meine Kinder, keine Angst zu haben, denn wo Haydn ist, kann nicht Schaden, fallen.' ('My children, have no fear, for where Haydn is, no harm can fall.')

William Hazlitt, 1778–1830
'Well, I've had a happy life.'

Hazlitt was an English essayist, journalist and critic. In his later years he was plagued with extremely painful illness, which nobody seems to have diagnosed perfectly. Eternally in pain and heavily drugged with opium by his doctor, he spent his last days in a delirium and is said to have declared to Charles Lamb and his son, 'Well, I've had a happy life.'

Georg Friedrich Wilhelm Hegel, 1770–1831
'Immer nur Du hast mich verstanden ... und Sie haben es falsch.'

Rector of the University of Berlin, teacher and philosopher. He seems to have died of a gastro-intestinal disease, although the physicians said it was cholera. One version of his final words is that he said to his favourite student,

'Immer nur Du hast mich verstanden ... und Sie haben es falsch,' ('Only you have ever understood me ... and you got it wrong') and another is that he said, 'And he didn't understand me.'

Heinrich Heine, 1797–1856
'Dieu me pardonnera. C'est son métier.'

Born in Dusseldorf, he was a German Jew who spent the last twenty-five years of his life as an expatriate in Paris. He was a poet, journalist, essayist, and literary critic. His health deteriorated in May 1848 with what turned out to be chronic lead poisoning and spent the next eight years in his bed. He died on 15 February 1856. His last words were, 'Dieu me pardonnera. C'est son métier.' ('God will pardon me. That's his line of work.')

Thomas Hobbes, 1588–1679
'A great leap in the dark.'

One of the founders of modern political philosophy. During the English Civil War, he wrote *Leviathan*, in which he set out his doctrine of the foundation of states and legitimate government. In October 1679, Hobbes suffered a bladder disorder, which was followed by a paralytic stroke from which he died on 4 December 1679. He is said to have uttered the last words, 'A great leap in the dark,' in his final moments.

A. E. Housman, 1859–1936
'I shall have to repeat that on the Golden Floor.'

English classical scholar and poet who wrote the poems *A Shropshire Lad*. He died at his home in Cambridge aged seventy-seven. It seems that his doctor told him a joke just before he died and his response, 'That is indeed very good. I shall have to repeat that on the Golden Floor,' proved to be his final words.

Robert E. Howard, 1906–1936
'The feast is over and the lamps expire.'

Suicide note by the American author, who wrote pulp fiction and who died on 11 June 1936. 'All fled – all done, so lift me on the pyre; The feast is over, and the lamps expire.'

Elbert Hubbard, 1856–1915
'There does not seem to be anything to do.'

American writer, publisher, artist, and philosopher, born in Hudson, Illinois. On 1 May 1915, the Hubbards boarded the RMS *Lusitania* in New York City. On 7 May, while at sea 11 miles (18 km) off the Old Head of Kinsale, Ireland, it was torpedoed and sunk by the German U-boat *U-20*.

A survivor of the sinking was one Ernest C. Cowper, who wrote to Elbert's son, Elbert Hubbard II, reporting on the death of his parents. It seems that they were in the habit of walking the deck with arms linked and, with no apparent care in the world, this is what they did as the liner went down. As Cowper passed the couple, carrying a baby to a lifeboat, Elbert said, 'Well, Jack, they have got us. They are a damn sight worse than I ever thought they were.'

As Cowper prepared to jump off the ship, he asked the Hubbards what they were going to do. Elbert responded, 'There does not seem to be anything to do.' He turned with his wife, entered a room on the top deck and closed the door behind him.

Victor Hugo, 1802–1885
'Je vois la lumière noire.'

Commonly regarded as one of the greatest and best-known French writers. Among his better-known works are *Les Misérables* (1862) and *Notre-Dame de Paris* (1831), known in English as *The Hunchback of Notre-Dame*. He died from pneumonia on 22 May 1885 at the age of eighty-three. He was not only revered as an author, he was seen as a statesman who shaped the Third Republic and democracy in France. More than two million people joined his funeral procession in Paris. He shares a crypt in the Panthéon with Alexandre Dumas and Émile Zola.

There are several alternative versions of his last words, 'Je vois la lumière noire.' ('I see black light.')

Another source claims that he said, 'Combien il est difficile de mourir.' ('How difficult it is to die.') His final written words were, 'Aimer, c'est agir.' ('To love is to act.') This last statement had some real meaning. He was a renowned lover who is said to have last had a woman on 5 April 1885.

Aldous Huxley, 1894–1963
'LSD, 100 µg, intramuscular.'

English writer and intellectual from Godalming in Surrey. He wrote *Brave New World* and *Doors of Perception* along with many other novels and short stories. He moved to Los Angeles in 1937 and remained there until he died. On his deathbed, unable to speak, Huxley made a written request to his wife Laura for 'LSD, 100 μg, intramuscular'. According to her account of his death, she obliged with an injection at 11:45 a.m. and a second one a few hours later; Huxley died aged sixty-nine, at 5:20 p.m. on 22 November 1963.

Henry James, 1843–1916
'So here it is at last, the distinguished thing!'

American-born writer who lived in England for some time. He became a British citizen as a declaration of loyalty to his adopted country and in protest against America's refusal to enter the war. He had a stroke on 2 December 1915. He was seriously ill when he was awarded the Order of Merit, bestowed on 1 January 1916. His health continued to decline and he died in London on 28 February 1916. His last words are popularly recorded as, 'So here it is at last, the distinguished thing!'

Dr Samuel Johnson, 1709–1784
'Bear my remembrance to your master.'

English writer who was a devout Anglican and dedicated Tory. He was extremely distinguished in his field and had a lasting impact on the language when he produced *A Dictionary of English Language*. He had disconcerting tics and mannerisms which, only latterly, were recognised as probable signs of Tourette's syndrome.

On 13 December 1784, Johnson met with two people: a young woman, Miss Morris, whom Johnson blessed, and Francesco Sastres, an Italian teacher, who was given some of Johnson's final words – 'Iam moriturus.' ('I who am about to die.') Shortly afterwards he fell into a coma and died.

An alternative account states that he said, 'Attend, Francis, to the salvation of your soul, which is the object of greatest importance.' He then responded to Miss Morris's request that he should give her his blessing. He did, saying, 'God bless you my dear.' Then to Cawston, the servant of William Wyndham, MP, 'Bear my remembrance to your master.'

James Joyce, 1882–1941
'Does nobody understand?'

Irish novelist and poet, known for his major work, *Ulysses*. In his early twenties he emigrated to continental Europe permanently, living variously in Trieste, Paris and Zurich. Despite this, almost all of his work is focused on Dublin. He is recorded as saying, 'For myself, I always write about Dublin, because if I can get to the heart of Dublin I can get to the heart of all the cities of the world. In the particular is contained the universal.'

On 11 January 1941, he was operated on for a perforated ulcer. He appeared to be recovering from the operation but relapsed the following day and fell into a coma. He awoke in the early hours of 13 January 1941, and asked for a nurse to call his wife and son before losing consciousness again. Those were probably his final words because he died fifteen minutes later. It is hard to verify the widely accepted idea that his final words were, 'Does nobody understand?'

Terry Alan Kath, 1946–1978
'Don't worry, it's not loaded.'

The original guitarist for the rock band Chicago. Around 5 p.m. on 23 January 1978, after a party at roadie/band technician Don Johnson's home in Woodland Hills, Los Angeles, Kath took an unloaded .38 revolver and put it to his head, pulling the trigger several times on the empty chambers. Kath had an absolute fascination for guns and he was warned to be careful. Kath then picked up a semiautomatic 9 mm pistol and said to Johnson, 'Don't worry, it's not loaded.' After showing the empty magazine to Johnson, Kath replaced the magazine in the gun, put the gun to his temple, and pulled the trigger. There was a round in the chamber, and he died instantly.

John Maynard Keynes, 1883–1946
'I only wish I had drunk more champagne.'

Possibly the most influential economist of the twentieth century, Keynes was born in Cambridge and returned there as a scholar at King's College after education at Eton. He was openly homosexual but did eventually marry Lydia Lopokova, a well-known Russian ballerina.

He suffered a series of heart attacks, which started while he was in Georgia, USA, during negotiations for an Anglo-American loan, and it was a heart attack that finally killed him at his home in Sussex on 21 April 1946.

Many sources allege that his final words were, 'I only wish I had drunk more champagne.'

John Keats, 1795–1821
'Be firm and thank God, it has come.'

English romantic poet. During February 1820 Keats displayed symptoms of tuberculosis, with two lung haemorrhages. He lost a great deal of blood and was further bled by the doctor. His doctors recommended that he should move to Italy with his friend Joseph Severn. Severn nursed him but the path was steadily downhill and it is this friend who reported the final words. 'Severn – I – lift me up, for I am dying. I shall die easy. Don't be frightened. Be firm and thank God, it has come.'

Timothy Leary, 1920–1996
'Beautiful.'

This is one of the few examples of final words that can be verified because his death was videotaped for posterity at his request. He was an American psychologist and writer who believed in using psychedelic drugs for psychotherapy. During the 1960s and 1970s, Leary was arrested regularly and was held captive in many different prisons around the world. President Richard Nixon once described Leary as 'the most dangerous man in America'.

He died on 31 May 1996 at the age of seventy-five. During his final moments, he said, 'Why not?' to his son Zachary. He uttered the phrase repeatedly and died soon after. His last word was, according to Zachary Leary, 'Beautiful.'

Franz Lehar, 1870–1948
'Ja, ja, mein liebes Kind, jetzt kommt der Tod.'

An Austro-Hungarian composer best known for his operettas, notably *The Merry Widow*. He died near Salzburg and his last words were, 'Jetzt habe ich mit allem irdischen Geschäft, und höchste Zeit fertig zu. Ja, ja, mein liebes Kind, jetzt kommt der Tod.' ('Now I have finished with all earthly business, and high time too. Yes, yes, my dear child. Now comes death.')

John Lennon, MBE, 1940–1980
'Life is what happens while you are busy making other plans.'

An English singer and songwriter who rose to fame as a founder member of the Beatles. At around 10:50 p.m. on 8 December 1980, Lennon and his wife, Yoko Ono, were returning to their New York apartment when a gunman, later identified as Mark Chapman, shot Lennon in the back four times. Lennon was taken to the nearby Roosevelt Hospital and was pronounced dead on arrival. Earlier that evening, Lennon had autographed a copy of *Double Fantasy* for Chapman. Because of the circumstances, no one apart from Yoko Ono can claim to know his final words. Nevertheless, one of his amusing final statements in writing was, 'Life is what happens while you are busy making other plans.'

Wyndham Lewis, 1884–1957
'Mind your own business.'

English painter and author who fought in the First World War as a second lieutenant in the Royal Artillery. In 1917 he was appointed as an official war artist for both the Canadian and British governments. A pituitary tumour which had caused him to go blind after 1951 ended his artistic career, though he was able to continue writing. His final words were, 'Mind your own business.'

Vachel Lindsay, 1879–1931
'They tried to get me – I got them first.'

An American poet who became known as 'the Prairie Troubadour' in the early twentieth century.

Despite fame and fortune, he was increasingly desperate for money. With his health failing after a six-month road trip, Lindsay became deeply depressed and, on 5 December 1931, committed suicide by drinking a bottle of Lysol. His last words were, 'They tried to get me - I got them first!'

Missak Manouchian, 1906–1944

'J'ai 15,000 francs dans la valise de la rue de Plaisance. Si vous pouvez l'obtenir, payez toutes mes dettes et donnez le reste à l'Arménie. MM.'
A French-Armenian poet and militant communist, who became well known for his leadership in the French Resistance.

He was executed by a Nazi firing squad on 21 February 1944 in Paris. His final letter, which is widely published, read,

My dear Melinée, my beloved little orphan, in a few hours I will no longer be of this world. We are going to be executed today at 3:00. This is happening to me like an accident in my life; I don't believe it, but I nevertheless know that I will never see you again.

What can I write you? Everything inside me is confused, yet clear at the same time. I joined the Army of Liberation as a volunteer, and I die within inches of victory and the final goal. I wish for happiness for all those who will survive and taste the sweetness of the freedom and peace of tomorrow. I'm sure that the French people, and all those who fight for freedom, will know how to honour our memory with dignity. At the moment of death, I proclaim that I have no hatred for the German people, or for anyone at all; everyone will receive what he is due, as punishment and as reward. The German people, and all other people, will live in peace and brotherhood after the war, which will not last much longer. Happiness for all ... I have one profound regret, and that's of not having made you happy; I would so much have liked to have a child with you, as you always wished. So I'd absolutely like you to marry after the war, and, for my happiness, to have a child and, to fulfill my last wish, marry someone who will make you happy. All my goods and all my affairs, I leave them to you and to my nephews. After the war you can request your right to a war pension as my wife, for I die as a regular soldier in the French army of liberation. With the help of friends who'd like to honor me, you should publish my poems and writings that are worth being read. If possible, you should take my memory to my parents in Armenia. I will soon die with 23 of my comrades, with the courage and the serenity of a man with a peaceful conscience; for, personally, I've done no one ill, and if I have, it was without hatred. Today is sunny. It's in looking at the sun and the beauties of nature that I loved so much that I will say farewell to life and to all of you, my beloved wife, and my beloved friends. I forgive all those who did me evil, or who wanted to do so, with the exception of he who betrayed us to redeem his skin, and those who sold us out. I ardently kiss you, as well as your sister and all those who know me, near and far; I hold you all against my heart. Farewell. Your friend, your comrade, your husband, Manouchian Michel

P.S. I have 15,000 francs in the valise on the Rue de Plaisance. If you can get it, pay off all my debts and give the rest to Armenia. MM.

Karl Marx, 1818–1883
'Go on, get out. Last words are for fools who haven't said enough.'

German philosopher whose work helped to create the socialist movement. He is also recognised as a leading economist. He published numerous books, of which the most notable were *Das Kommunistische Manifest* (1848) and *Das Kapital* (1867–1894). His name is always linked with fellow revolutionary socialist Friedrich Engels.

Marx developed a catarrh which contributed to the bronchitis and pleurisy that killed him in London on 14 March 1883. The last recorded words were to his housekeeper, who urged him to tell her his last words so that she could record them for posterity. He replied, 'Go on, get out. Last words are for fools who haven't said enough.'

W. Somerset Maugham, 1874–1965
'Dying is a very dull, dreary affair. And my advice to you is to have nothing whatever to do with it.'

British playwright and novelist. He was reputedly the highest-paid author during the 1930s. During the First World War, he served with the Red Cross and in the ambulance corps, before being recruited into the British Secret Intelligence Service in 1916. He worked in Switzerland and Russia before the Bolshevik Revolution of 1917. Maugham's public view of his abilities remained modest. Toward the end of his career he described himself as 'in the very first row of the second-raters'.

He died in Nice and, although there is nothing to authenticate it, his last words were said to be, 'Dying is a very dull, dreary affair. And my advice to you is to have nothing whatever to do with it.'

Glen Miller, 1904–1944
'Hey! Where the hell are the parachutes?'

Big-band musician of the 1930s and 1940s. Miller spent his last night, 14 December 1944, at the Hall in Milton Ernest, near Bedford. The next day he was to fly from England to Paris to play for the Army. His plane departed from RAF Twinwood Farm on the outskirts of Bedford and disappeared while flying over the English Channel. No trace of the aircrew, passengers or plane has ever been found. Miller's status is 'missing in action'.

As he boarded his plane to Paris he reportedly asked the question of one Colonel Baesell, 'Hey, where the hell are the parachutes?' An official replied, 'What's the matter, Miller? Do you want to live forever?'

Lady Mary Wortley Montagu, 1689–1762
'It's all been very interesting.'

Born in London, the daughter of the 5th Earl of Kingston-upon-Hull. Against her father's guidance, she eloped with Edward Wortley Montagu, who became an MP three years later. In 1716 he was appointed as ambassador to Instanbul. This experience provided the opportunity for her to write about her travels and she proved to be an amusing author with an eye for the interesting detail.

Her beauty was marred by a severe attack of smallpox while she was still a young woman, and she later pioneered the practice of inoculation in England, an initiative which was strongly resisted by the medical profession, who regarded it as 'an oriental practice'.

For reasons that are not wholly clear, Lady Mary's relationship with her husband became distant. In 1736 she became infatuated with an Italian writer and hoped to live with him in Italy. She set off to do so, but he failed to meet her, having been called to Berlin by Kaiser Frederick II.

She died of cancer while staying with her daughter, Mary, who was married to the Earl of Bute, the then Prime Minister. Her last words were, 'It's all been very interesting.'

Wolfgang Amadeus Mozart, 1756–1791
'Der Geschmack des Todes ist auf meinen Lippen ... Ich fühle mich etwas, das ist nicht von dieser Erde.'

An Austrian child prodigy with the keyboard and violin, he was composing by the age of five. He was a prolific composer and to this day remains one of the most popular classical musicians. Despite the patronage of many, he experienced constant financial problems, backed by ill health. He was nursed in his final illness by his wife and her youngest sister, and was attended by the family doctor, Thomas Franz Closset. Throughout the illness, he was occupied with the task of finishing his unfinished Requiem K626. His last words were reported to be, 'Der Geschmack des Todes ist auf meinen Lippen ... Ich fühle mich etwas, das ist nicht von dieser Erde.' ('The taste of death is upon my lips ... I feel something that is not of this earth.')

Eugene O'Neill, 1888–1953
'I knew it. I knew it. Born in a hotel room and, God damn it, died in a hotel room.'

An Irish American playwright and Nobel laureate in Literature, O'Neill died in Room 401 of the Sheraton Hotel on Bay State Road in Boston, on 27 November 1953, whispering, 'I knew it. I knew it. Born in a hotel room and, God damn it, died in a hotel room.'

Boris Pasternak, 1890–1959
'Don't forget to open the window tomorrow.'

He was the author of *Doctor Zhivago*, a novel which the Soviet authorities denied him the right to publish. The book was published in 1957 in Italy. Pasternak was awarded the Nobel Prize for Literature in 1958, which enraged the leaders of the Soviet Union. The authorities stated that if he went to collect the award, he would not be allowed back into the Soviet Union. Pasternak was forced to turn down the award. He wrote to the Nobel committee saying that it was not his decision, but that of the state.

In the end, the stance of the authorities damaged the credibility of the Soviet Union. He remains a major figure in Russian literature.

Knowing that death was close, he summoned his sons, and asked them who would suffer the most because of his death. His last words were, 'I can't hear very well. And there's a mist in front of my eyes. But it will go away, won't it? Don't forget to open the window tomorrow.'

Another commentator claims that he said, 'Goodbye. Why am I haemorrhaging?'

Pietro Perugino, 1446–1523
'Sono curioso di vedere cosa succede nel mondo accanto a uno che muore unshriven.'

An Italian Renaissance painter of the Umbrian school. Raphael was his most famous pupil and his major works hang in Washington DC,

Florence, Paris, Rome, Munich, St Petersburg, Bologna, Fano, Caen, Sao Paulo, London and Birmingham.

He was at Fontignano in 1523 when he died of the plague. Like other plague victims, he was hastily buried in an unconsecrated field, the precise spot unknown. He is alleged to have said, 'Sono curioso di vedere cosa succede nel mondo accanto a uno che muore unshriven.' ('I am curious to see what happens in the next world to one who dies unshriven.')

Hillary 'Harry' St John Philby, 1885–1960
'Take me away, I'm bored here.'

Arabist, explorer, writer and intelligence officer. He was fluent in all of the languages of Pakistan, and spoke Persian and some Arabic. His distant cousin, Bernard Montgomery, was best man at his first wedding. Later he married an Arab woman from Saudi Arabia. His one son was Kim Philby, who joined the Secret Intelligence Service and betrayed the country by becoming a double agent for the Soviet Union. He also had three daughters.

Gordon Corera's excellent book *The Art of Betrayal* related how the two Philby men lunched with a friend before St John went home to have a nap, after which he attempted to seduce the wife of one of the embassy staff in a night club. He had a heart attack that night and died the following morning. His last words were, 'Take me away, I'm bored here.'

Edith Piaf, 1915–1963
'Chaque chose d'idiot foutu que vous faites dans la vie, vous payez.'

Born Édith Giovanna Gassion, she was a French singer who was named after Edith Cavell, who was executed by the Germans in 1915 for helping Allied soldiers to escape from Belgium. She was widely known as La Môme Piaf (The Little Sparrow) and was probably France's most important international star.

She died of liver cancer at the age of forty-seven at her villa on the French Riviera, on 11 October 1963. She had been bedridden for several months and was often unconscious. Her last words were, 'Chaque chose d'idiot foutu que vous faites dans la vie, vous payez.' ('Every damn fool thing you do in this life, you pay for.')

Pablo Picasso, 1881–1973
'Buvez-moi, boire à ma santé, vous savez que je ne peux plus boire.'

A Spanish artist with ability in many fields who spent most of his adult life in France. Arguably he was one of the most influential artists of the twentieth century, and he was a co-founder of the Cubist movement. He experimented freely with different art forms and his style changed several times during the course of his prolific artistic life.

He died on 8 April 1973 in Mougins, France, while he and his wife Jacqueline had friends for dinner. His final words were, 'Buvez-moi, boire à ma santé, vous savez que je ne peux plus boire.' ('Drink to me, drink to my health, you know I can't drink any more.')

Edgar Allan Poe, 1809–1849
'Reynolds.'

An American author and literary critic who is credited with being the inventor of detective fiction. His tales of mystery and the macabre were matched by his less well-known humour, satire and hoax stories. As a critic he could be relentless and engaged in particular in a campaign against Henry Longfellow, the author of *The Song of Hiawatha*.

On 3 October 1849, Poe was found on the streets of Baltimore 'in great distress, and in need of immediate assistance'. He was taken to the Washington Medical College, where he died on Sunday, 7 October 1849. Nobody knows why or how Poe came to be in such difficulty. He himself was never coherent long enough to explain what happened. Strangely he was wearing clothes that were not his own. He is said to have repeatedly called out the name 'Reynolds' in the hours before he died. Some sources say Poe's final words were, 'Lord help my poor soul.'

Alexander Pope, 1688–1744
'Here am I, dying of a hundred good symptoms.'

An eighteenth-century English poet, he completed a translation of the works of Homer, first the *Iliad* in 1715-1720, followed by the *Odyssey* in 1726. He was famous for his use of the heroic couplet, and is said to be the third-most frequently quoted writer in *The Oxford Dictionary of Quotations*, after Shakespeare and Tennyson.

Pope's health had never been good and he was well prepared for death. He died at his home in Twickenham, surrounded by his family and friends on 30 May 1744. His final words were, 'Here am I, dying of a hundred good symptoms.'

William Sydney Porter, 1862–1910
'Turn up the lights, I don't want to go home in the dark.'

Better known by his pen name, O. Henry, he was an American writer of excellent short stories. But he did have a chequered career and was arrested for embezzlement after a federal audit at the First National Bank of Austin. He fled the country, despite his father-in-law posting bail for him, leaving his wife in Austin. When he learned that she was gravely ill, he returned to Austin where she duly died of tuberculosis. He surrendered to the court and was later sentenced to five years in jail. He had fourteen stories published while he was in prison, but his most prolific period happened after his release in 1901.

Porter was a heavy drinker, and his health deteriorated markedly in 1908, which affected his writing. His last words on 4 June 1910, according to his 1916 biographer, Charles Alphonso Smith, were, 'Turn up the lights, I don't want to go home in the dark.'

Elvis Presley, 1935–1977
'I won't.'

American singer. One of the most popular singers of the twentieth century, he is commonly known by the single name Elvis or 'the King.'

Presley's last four years were a catalogue of drug abuse. He put on a huge amount of weight and became incoherent on stage. The fans were incensed. He was due to fly out of Memphis on the evening of 16 August 1977, to begin another tour. That afternoon his girlfriend, Ginger Alden, discovered him unconscious on his bathroom floor. Attempts to revive him failed, and death was officially pronounced at 3.30 p.m. at Baptist Memorial Hospital. There is a story that Alden saw him going to the lavatory and said to him, 'Don't go to sleep in there,' to which he allegedly replied, 'I won't.'

The last thing he said at his final press conference was, 'I hope I haven't bored you.'

Francois Rabelais, 1494–1553
'Je dois beaucoup, je n'ai rien, je laisse le reste aux pauvres.'

French monk, scholar, writer and doctor. His writing involved fantasy, satire, the grotesque, bawdy jokes, particularly double-entendres, and songs.

He was often very short of money, which accounts for one version of his final words: 'Je dois beaucoup, je n'ai rien, je laisse le reste aux pauvres.' ('I owe much; I have nothing; the rest I leave to the poor.') Another source suggests that he said, 'Je vais chercher un grand peut-être.' ('I am going to seek a great perhaps.')

George Bernard Shaw, 1856–1950
'I'm going to die.'

The playwright, who wrote more than sixty plays, had a most irregular education because he disliked organised training. This proved no impediment to his longer term success, for he was awarded the Nobel Prize for Literature in 1925. He died on 2 November 1950 from renal problems which were not helped by the injuries he received when he fell off a ladder.

His final words were, 'Sister, you're trying to keep me alive as an old curiosity, but I'm done, I'm finished. I'm going to die.' Another source reports that he said, 'Dying is easy, comedy is hard.' Yet another source insists, 'Life levels all men. Death reveals the eminent.'

Adam Smith, 1723–1790
'I believe we must adjourn the meeting to some other place.'

Scottish moral philosopher and one of the key figures of the Scottish Enlightenment. At the age of twenty-five he began lecturing at Edinburgh University and later taught logic at Glasgow University.

His most important work was *An Inquiry into the Nature and Causes of the Wealth of Nations* (1776), which is more commonly known as *The Wealth of Nations*.

He was an unusual character, given to talking aloud to himself and living with his mother until she died, a mere six years before he did. He never married, was incredibly absent-minded and experienced phantom illnesses, but he is still recognised as the father of modern economics.

He endured a painful illness and died in Panmure House, his late mother's home, on 17 July 1790. His final words were, 'I believe we must adjourn the meeting to some other place.' Some sources claim that he said that he was disappointed that he had not achieved more.

Socrates, 469–399 BC
'Crito, I owe a cock to Asclepius. Please pay it and don't forget it.'

An Athenian philosopher credited as one of the founders of Western philosophy. He was put on trial for corrupting the minds of the youth of Athens. He was found guilty and sentenced to die by drinking hemlock.

His friends urged him to escape, but he declined to do so for three reasons: firstly, he believed that flight would indicate a fear of death. Secondly, he judged that his teaching would fare no better in any other country, and thirdly, he accepted the laws of the state. After drinking the poison, he was instructed to walk around until his legs felt numb. After he lay down, the man who administered the poison pinched his foot; Socrates could no longer feel his legs. The numbness slowly crept up his body until it reached his heart. Shortly before his death, Socrates spoke his last words. 'Crito, I owe a cock to Asclepius. Please pay it and don't forget it.'

Gertrude Stein, 1874–1946
'In that case, what is the question?'

American novelist and poet who was born in Pittsburgh but lived for many years in Paris and died there. Diagnosed with stomach cancer, she was being wheeled into the operating theatre for surgery and asked, 'What is the answer?' Nobody said anything, so she asked, 'In that case, what is the question?'

Lytton Strachey, 1880–1932
'If this is dying, then I don't think much of it.'

A founding member of the Bloomsbury Group and author of *Eminent Victorians*. He had a relationship with John Maynard Keynes, who was also a member of the Bloomsbury Set.

He died at Ham Spray House, Marlborough, of undiagnosed stomach cancer. It is said that his final words were, 'If this is dying, then I don't think much of it.'

Jonathan Swift, 1667–1745
'Ah, a German and a genius! A prodigy, admit him!'

An Anglo-Irish satirist and essayist. He became Dean of St Patrick's Cathedral, Dublin, and is widely known as the author of *Gulliver's Travels*.

Some sources say that his final words on hearing of the arrival of Handel were, 'Ah, a German and a genius! A prodigy, admit him!'

His epitaph in Latin in St Patrick's Cathedral, Dublin, was written by the man himself.

Peter Ilyich Tchaikovsky, 1840–1893
'Я считаю, что смерть.'

A prolific and highly popular Russian composer whose music included symphonies, operas, ballets and chamber music.

In October 1893 he died, nine days after conducting the premiere of his Sixth Symphony in St Petersburg. The cause was probably cholera, although many suspected that he committed suicide. His final words were, 'Я считаю, что смерть.' ('I believe it's death.')

Sara Teasdale, 1884–1933
'It is strange how often a heart must be broken before the years can make it wise.'

American poet from Missouri. The popular record is that her poem 'I Shall Not Care' was her suicide note to a lover who left her. The poem reads, 'When I am dead, and over me bright April/ Shakes out her rain drenched hair/ Tho you should lean above me broken hearted/ I shall not care. For I shall have peace. As leafey trees are peaceful/ When rain bends down the bough. And I shall be more silent and cold hearted/ Than you are now.'

Unfortunately the poem was published in 1915, eighteen years before her suicide. One possibility is that she left a note of another of her acknowledged statements: 'It is strange how often a heart must be broken before the years can make it wise.'

William Makepeace Thackeray, 1811–1863
'Bring me a brandy and water, if you please.'

English novelist famous for his satirical works, particularly *Vanity Fair*, a portrait of English society. He rather enjoyed writing about rogues and was forceful with his attacks on high society.

His health worsened during the 1850s. He felt he had lost his creativity and made matters worse by overeating, drinking and avoiding exercise. He was absolutely addicted to spicy peppers, which caused further damage to his digestion. On 23 December 1863, after returning from dining out, he had a stroke and was found dead the following morning.

At any time he may well have said, 'Bring me a brandy and water, if you please,' but there is no evidence that these were his final words.

Dylan Thomas, 1914–1953
'I've had eighteen straight whiskies. I think that's the record.'

Welsh poet and writer who is widely known for *Under Milk Wood*.

He died when on a working visit to New York. Many sources claim that his final words were, 'I've had eighteen straight whiskies. I think that's the record.' In fact he said this on the night of 3 November 1953. He was desperately ill but still talking until 5 November when an ambulance was called to collect him from the Hotel Chelsea. He was then comatose and did not regain consciousness before he died on 9 November. Nobody recorded any memorable statements between 3 and 5 November.

Henry David Thoreau, 1817–1862
'Now comes good sailing ... moose ... Indian ... '

American author, poet and philosopher. His health disintegrated steadily over a number of years and he used his time to set his affairs in order. During his final weeks, his aunt Louisa asked him, 'Have you made your peace with God?'

'I did not know we had ever quarrelled.'

'But aren't you concerned about the next world?' she asked.

'One world at a time,' he replied. His final sentence from his sickbed was 'Now comes good sailing ... moose ... Indian ... '

James Thurber, 1894–1961
'God bless. God damn.'

Born in Ohio, Thurber was an American humorist and writer of amusing short stories, many of which were published in the *New Yorker* magazine. He had a stroke in 1961, which was then complicated by pneumonia. According to his second wife, Helen, his final words were, 'God bless. God damn.'

William Tindale, 1494–1536
'Lord, open the King of England's eyes.'

The translator of the modern English Bible, who with William Shakespeare was responsible for changing our language and culture. In 1536 he was tried in Belgium for heresy and was executed by strangulation. His final words were, 'Lord, open the King of England's eyes.'

Leo Tolstoy, 1828–1910
'Даже в долине смертной тени, два и два не делают шесть.'

Possibly one of the greatest of Russian writers, he died of pneumonia at Astapovo train station, after falling ill when he left home at the dead of night in the middle of the winter. He had been playing with the idea of leaving home, to separate from his wife and renounce his aristocratic lifestyle. His night-time departure was an apparent attempt to escape unannounced from the jealous tirades of his wife Sonia. His final words were, 'Запрашивать, всегда искать.' ('To seek, always to seek.') One story has it that he was urged to return to the fold of the Russian Orthodox Church. His response was, 'Даже в долине смертной тени, два и два не делают шесть.' ('Even in the valley of the shadow of death, two and two do not make six.')

Joseph (J. M. W.) Turner, 1775–1851
'The sun is God.'

The British Romantic landscape painter and watercolourist who was the son of a barber and wig maker. He became known as 'the artist of light', and is now regarded as the artist who elevated landscape painting to greater prominence. In his personal life, he had few friends and was regarded as something of an eccentric. He never married but is believed to have been the father of two daughters with a woman called Sarah Danby.

The Earl of Egremont frequently asked Turner to stay at Petworth House, which still boasts the many landscape scenes he painted there.

He died in the house of his mistress, Sophia Caroline Booth, in Cheyne Walk in Chelsea on 19 December 1851. He is said to have uttered the last words, 'The sun is God.'

Richard Versalle, 1932–1996
'Too bad you can only live so long.'

American operatic tenor from Michigan, whose first job was as a submariner in the US Navy. During the world premiere of Janacek's *The Makropulos Case* at New York's Metropolitan Opera, he was halfway up a ladder on stage, playing the part of Vitek, an elderly law clerk. He sang the fateful words, 'Too bad you can only live so long.' He then had a heart attack and fell off the ladder, dead.

Leonardo da Vinci, 1452–1519
'Ho offeso Dio e l'umanità, perché il mio lavoro non ha raggiunto la qualità che dovrebbe avere.'

An Italian Renaissance polymath. His range of skills, interests and ability was breathtaking. He was a painter (for which he is most well known), sculptor, architect, musician, mathematician, engineer, inventor, anatomist, geologist, cartographer, botanist, and writer. Some may say he was a genius.

Leonardo died at Clos Lucé, Amboise, on 2 May 1519. This had been his official residence since 1516 when Francois I offered it to him for his work. The chateau is close to the royal Chateau d'Amboise and is connected by an underground passage. The legend is that Francois had become a close friend and held Leonardo's head in his arms as he died. There is no formal record of his final words, although there are three broadly similar versions published; one of these is, 'Ho offeso Dio e l'umanità, perché il mio lavoro non ha raggiunto la qualità che dovrebbe avere.' ('I have offended God and mankind because my work did not reach the quality it should have.')

Voltaire, 1694–1778
'Je n'ai pas le temps de faire d'autres ennemis.'

Voltaire was the nom de plume of François-Marie Arouet, a French writer, historian and philosopher famous for his attacks on the Catholic Church. The adopted name is an anagram of 'AROVET LI', composed of the Latinised spelling of his surname, Arouet, and the initial letters of 'le jeune'.

Exiled to England in 1726, Voltaire returned to Paris in 1729. Over the next forty-nine years he lived in Holland, Germany and Switzerland, finally returning to Paris in 1778 after a twenty-year gap to see the opening of his latest tragedy, *Irene*. The long journey took its toll on him and he believed he was about to die. His words were noted: 'Je meurs en adorant Dieu, en aimant mes amis, pas haïr mes ennemis, et détestant la superstition.' ('I die adoring God, loving my friends, not hating my enemies, and detesting superstition.')

But he survived and did not actually die until 30 May 1778. There are many conflicting stories about his final words, but the favourite account is that on being exhorted to renounce sin and the devil, he exclaimed, 'Je n'ai pas le temps de faire d'autres ennemis.' ('I haven't time to make any more enemies.')

Sam Ward, 1814–1884
'I think I'm going to give up the ghost.'

US poet and author who enjoyed good living. He became known as the 'King of the Lobby' because he created a form of social lobbying which relied upon good food, wine and conversation. He always wrote amusingly about his life and experience, and was noted for his hilarious account *Sam Ward in the Gold Rush*.

He lived extremely well, largely on other people's money. Despite being given an enormous sum of money by James Keene, whom he had supported in the Californian gold fields, he lost the lot in a failed investment. He left America and dropped into London before moving on the Italy, where he died near Naples after dictating a light-hearted letter. His final words were, 'I think I'm going to give up the ghost.'

Auberon Waugh, 1939–2001
'Have they sacked Dominic Lawson yet?'

English journalist and author who was the son of Evelyn Waugh. He was noted mainly for his diary in *Private Eye*. A lifelong smoker, he died of heart disease at the relatively youthful age of sixty-one. His final words were said to be, 'Have they sacked Dominic Lawson yet?'

H. G. Wells, 1866–1946
'Go away. I'm alright.'

English novelist best known for his science fiction. In his preface to the 1941 edition of *The War in the Air*, Wells stated that his epitaph should be, 'I told you so. You *damned* fools.' There is some dispute about where he actually died in London, but the cause was a heart attack. Apparently his final words were, 'Go away. I'm alright.'

Walt Whitman, 1819–1892
'I can't breathe. Turn me over.'

American poet and journalist who also worked as a teacher and a government clerk. He had a stroke in 1873 but recovered and lived an active life in New Jersey. In 1891 he commissioned a granite mausoleum shaped like a house and visited it often during construction. In the last week of his life, he was too weak to feed himself but managed to write, 'I suffer all the time: I have no relief, no escape: it is monotony – monotony – monotony – in pain.'

The cause of death was officially listed as 'pleurisy of the left side, consumption of the right lung, general miliary tuberculosis and parenchymatous nephritis'. An autopsy found that his lungs had reduced to one-eighth of their normal breathing capacity, so it is small wonder that his last words were, 'I can't breathe. Turn me over.'

Oscar Wilde, 1854–1900
'Either that wallpaper goes, or I do.'

Irish poet and playwright who was the rage of London in the 1890s. He had a rapier wit and wonderful turn of phrase, but was vilified for his homosexuality, which landed him in Pentonville and Wandsworth prisons. Ultimately he died in a Paris garret, allegedly uttering the immortal words, 'Either that wallpaper goes, or I do,' which he did. Another deathbed quotation is also attributed to him: he asked for champagne to sip as he died, and as he sipped, he is reported to have said, 'Alas, I am dying beyond my means.'

The truth is a little more prosaic. He died of cerebral meningitis and was semi-comatose during his final hours. A friend, Robert Ross, called a priest to baptise Wilde into the Catholic Church. Father Cuthbert Dunne did his duty, noting that Wilde struggled to repeat the priest's words after him.

Virginia Woolf, 1882–1941
'I don't think two people could have been happier than we have been.'

English modernist author. She experienced deep depression and eventually

committed suicide by filling her pockets with stones and walking into the River Ouse near her home. She left a note for her husband, which read, 'Dearest, I feel certain that I am going mad again. I feel we can't go through another of those terrible times. And I shan't recover this time. I begin to hear voices, and I can't concentrate. So I am doing what seems the best thing to do. You have given me the greatest possible happiness. You have been in every way all that anyone could be. I don't think two people could have been happier 'til this terrible disease came. I can't fight any longer. I know that I am spoiling your life, that without me you could work. And you will I know. You see I can't even write this properly. I can't read. What I want to say is I owe all the happiness of my life to you. You have been entirely patient with me and incredibly good. I want to say that – everybody knows it. If anybody could have saved me it would have been you. Everything has gone from me but the certainty of your goodness. I can't go on spoiling your life any longer. I don't think two people could have been happier than we have been.'

William Wordsworth, 1770–1850
'Please excuse me if I fall asleep.'

English Romantic poet. He was appointed Poet Laureate in 1843 on the death of Robert Southey, but is the only person to have fulfilled the role without writing any official poetry.

He died of pleurisy as he was being read to (not one of his own works) and his final words were, 'Please excuse me if I fall asleep.'

Sergei Yesenin, 1895–1925
'Там нет ничего нового в умирающих сейчас; Хотя гостиная нет более новых.'

One of the most popular and well-known Russian lyrical poets of the twentieth century. He was an alcoholic who experienced mental health problems which led to him being hospitalised for a month before his death. On being released, he went to the Hotel Angleterre in Moscow, cut his wrist and wrote a farewell poem in his own blood. It is said that he hanged himself from the heating pipes on the ceiling of his room. The poem read, 'Goodbye, my friend, goodbye; My love, you are in my heart. It was preordained we should part; And be reunited by and by. Goodbye: no handshake to endure. Let's have no sadness-furrowed brow. There's nothing new in dying now; Though living is no newer.'

Actors, Performing Arts

Tallulah Bankhead, 1902–1968
'Codeine, Bourbon.'

American actress born in Alabama to a powerful Democratic family. She was famous not only as an actress, but also for her many affairs. She had flair and was the author of many excellent one-liners like, 'There is less to this than meets the eye.'

She had the reputation of being sexually available to anyone she found attractive and was credited with a string of affairs with men and women, the longest of which lasted one year. She died on 12 December 1968 in St Luke's Hospital, Manhattan, of emphysema and malnutrition. Her last words were reported to be, 'Codeine, Bourbon.'

P. T. Barnum, 1810–1891
'How were the receipts today at Madison Square Garden?'

Phineas Taylor Barnum, born in Bethel, Connecticut, started a small local business in his early twenties but swiftly decided to move on to the big city. Setting up shop in New York, he created a variety troupe called Barnum's Grand Scientific and Musical Theater. He then bought Scudder's American Museum. He used the museum to promote hoaxes and human curiosities such as 'General Tom Thumb.' He promoted the American tour of singer Jenny Lind and paid her $1,000 a night for 150 nights. Things went wrong financially in the 1850s but he persevered and became Mayor of Bridgeport, Connecticut. He did a great deal to improve public services and he enforced liquor and prostitution laws. He was a driving force in the creation of Bridgeport Hospital, founded in 1878, and was its first president.

But he is best known for becoming a great entrepreneur and showman. He had a stroke during a performance in 1890 and died on 7 April 1891. His last words were supposed to be, 'How were the receipts today at Madison Square Garden?'

Ethel Barrymore, 1879–1959
'Is everybody happy? I want everybody to be happy. I know I'm happy.'
The American actress was one of the Barrymore family of actors. She had many roles on stage and screen between 1895 and 1957. Her private life included some time in England, where it is said that Winston Churchill once proposed to her, although she never mentioned it. She eventually married Russell Colt, a descendant of the gunmaker Samuel Colt. It was not a happy marriage, although she gave birth to three children. The couple divorced in 1923.

She died of heart disease at her Hollywood home and is reported to have said, 'Is everybody happy? I want everybody to be happy. I know I'm happy.'

John Barrymore, 1882–1942
'You heard me, Mike.'
The American actor, who was married and divorced four times, collapsed while appearing on Rudy Vallee's radio show and died in his hospital room on 29 May 1942. One version of his final words is, 'Die? I should say not, dear fellow. No Barrymore would allow such a conventional thing to happen to him.'

Gene Fowler attributes different dying words to Barrymore in his biography *Good Night, Sweet Prince*. According to Fowler, John Barrymore tried to say something to his brother Lionel; Lionel asked him to repeat himself, and he simply replied, 'You heard me, Mike.'

Humphrey Bogart, 1899–1957
'Goodbye, Kid. Hurry back.'
American actor, seen by many as an icon of the American film industry. A heavy smoker and drinker, his health started to fail in the mid-1950s. He was diagnosed with cancer of the oesophagus, but surgery failed to stem the disease. On the night before he died, Katharine Hepburn and Spencer Tracy visited him at home. As they were leaving, Tracy patted Bogart on the shoulder and said, 'Goodnight, Bogie.' Bogart covered Tracy's hand with his own and said, 'Goodbye, Spence.' Tracy got the message.

Bogart soon fell into a coma from which he never revived, so it is not likely that the traditional list of his final words is accurate, although he probably expressed the sentiments at some time before he died. The favourite is, 'I should have switched from whisky to Martini', while another source quotes, 'I should never have switched from scotch to martinis'. William Barnes, in his book *Last Words of Notable People*, asserts that his last words were to his wife, Lauren Bacall. 'Goodbye, Kid. Hurry back.'

Lenny Bruce, 1925–1966
'Do you know where I can get any shit?'

American comedian and satirist. He tended to use obscene words and gestures which, combined with his use of drugs, constantly got him into trouble. He was banned from appearing in many cities in the USA, and in 1962 he was banned from appearing on stage in Sydney, Australia.

Allegedly his last words were, 'Do you know where I can get any shit?' but the fact is that no one recorded the information. On 3 August 1966, he was found dead in the bathroom of his Hollywood Hills home at 8825 W. Hollywood Boulevard. The official photo showed Bruce lying naked on the floor with drug equipment beside him.

Charley Chaplin, 1889–1977
'Why not? After all, it belongs to him.'

Sir Charles Spencer 'Charlie' Chaplin KBE was a British comic actor and filmmaker who rose to fame in the silent era. He lived in the USA for many years but his political views were resented by the US establishment and he was investigated by the FBI as a possible communist sympathiser. The USA decided they would not renew his visa, and he robustly decided that he no longer wished to live in the country, saying, 'I was fed up of America's insults and moral pomposity.'

In his later years, living near Geneva in Switzerland, he suffered a number of strokes, which made it difficult for him to communicate. His last words, therefore, were probably dreamed up by someone else. Apparently a priest said, 'May the Lord have mercy on your soul.'

Chaplin is reported to have replied, 'Why not? After all, it belongs to him.' The words are actually a quotation from his 1946 film *Monsieur Verdoux*.

Christine Chubbuck, 1944–1974
'You're about to see another first – an attempted suicide.'

An American television news reporter who struggled with depression and tried to kill herself in 1970. Her family was well aware, but her employers were not. She committed suicide during a live television broadcast in July 1974. She said, 'And now, in keeping with Channel 40's policy of always bringing you the latest in blood and guts, in living colour, you're about to see another first – an attempted suicide.' She revealed a revolver and shot herself.

Lou Costello, 1906–1959
'I think I'll be more comfortable.'

The comedian, who developed a double act with Bud Abbott. Despite many disagreements, they created a very successful partnership, making thirty-six films between 1940 and 1956.

Newspapers reported that he died of a heart attack in Beverly Hills on 3 March 1959. His final words were supposed to be, 'I think I'll be more comfortable.'

There is a claim that he died in the presence of friends and that his last words were, 'That was the best ice-cream soda I ever tasted.' Many commentators believe that this is a myth aimed at Costello's weight.

Joan Crawford, 1905–1977
'Damn it. Don't you dare ask God to help me.'

Born Lucille Fay LeSueur, she was an American actress. She married four times and was divorced three times. A heavy smoker and drinker, her health deteriorated to such an extent that she needed round-the-clock nursing in her New York apartment. Close to death, she is alleged to have remonstrated with her housekeeper, who had begun to pray aloud, saying, 'Damn it. Don't you dare ask God to help me.' She died of a heart attack.

Bing Crosby, 1903–1977
'That was a great game, fellas.'

American singer and actor who sold 500 million records. His biggest hit was Irving Berlin's 'White Christmas'. It was – even if it may not still be – the biggest-selling hit of all time, with sales of more than 50 million records.

Crosby loved sport and was a keen supporter and part-owner of the Pittsburgh Pirates. He was also a keen golfer. On 14 October 1977 he collapsed and died of a massive heart attack on the green after a round of eighteen holes of golf near Madrid where he and his Spanish golfing partner had just defeated their opponents. His last words were reported as, 'That was a great game, fellas.'

Rene Cutforth, 1909–1984
'Is that it then?'

British broadcaster and journalist who served in the Army during the Second World War. He was captured and spent time as a prisoner of war in Italy and Germany, returning to England in 1946 to join the BBC as a correspondent. Clive James called him 'a front man with background'.

His health failed in 1984 and, after three days in a coma at his home in Essex, he woke briefly and said to his loyal wife, 'Is that it then?' and died.

James Dean, 1931–1955
'My fun days are over.'

American film actor. He was the first actor to receive a posthumous Academy Award nomination for Best Actor.

His status and reputation was bound to spawn famous last words. Dean was driving his Porsche Spyder with a passenger, who was a factory-trained mechanic. They had already been stopped for speeding ninety minutes earlier. Sixty miles further on, Dean was 'testing' the speed limit again and overtaking a number of vehicles, allegedly at 85 mph. He may not have been responsible for the eventual collision with a Ford coupe. The two cars crashed almost head-on. Amazingly, the only fatality was James Dean, although his passenger had no memory of what immediately preceded the crash, so could not validate any final words.

Some say that Dean's last known words, uttered after his passenger told him to slow down, were, 'That guy's gotta stop ... He'll see us.' But there is no formal record of anyone saying anything and it is little more than speculation since the one viable witness couldn't remember anything.

Many sources claim that he said, 'My fun days are over,' shortly before his fatal car crash.

Isadora Duncan, 1877–1927
'Je vais à l'amour.'

An American dancer who is widely considered to be the founder of modern dance. She was flamboyant, notorious for her love affairs (with both sexes) and constantly in financial difficulties. She was also a communist and was exiled from her native land because of her political ideals.

Popular mythology has it that her final words, to her friend Mary Desti, were, 'Adieu, mes amis. Je vais a la gloire,' ('Adieu, my friends. I go to glory') spoken as she got into a roadster in Nice driven by a handsome French-Italian mechanic. She flung her long scarf around her neck in a dramatic gesture and when the car pulled away, the scarf caught in the spokes of the wheel and broke her neck.

The American novelist Glenway Wescott claimed that Desti had lied about Duncan's last words. Apparently Duncan actually said, 'Je vais à l'amour.' ('I am off to love.') Desti considered this embarrassing, so altered the words.

Douglas Fairbanks Snr, 1883–1939
'I never felt better.'

An American actor, screenwriter, director and producer. As an actor in silent movies, he normally played the role of the ebullient and energetic hero. He was also a clever businessman, and was a founding member of United Artists. He hosted the first Oscars ceremony in 1929. He and his wife, Mary Pickford, became Hollywood's stars and Fairbanks was referred to as 'The King of Hollywood', a nickname later acquired by Clark Gable. But he was unenthusiastic about 'the talkies' and his energy and athleticism began to decline because he was a heavy smoker.

In December 1939, at the age of fifty-six, Fairbanks had a heart attack and died later at his home in Santa Monica. By some accounts, he had been obsessively working out against medical advice, trying to regain his once-trim waistline. His last words were said to be, 'I never felt better.'

W. C. Fields, 1880–1946
'I'd rather be in Philadelphia.'

Born William Claude Dukenfield in Darby, Pennsylvania, he was a comedian, actor and writer. Fields developed a specific persona as a woman-hating, hard-drinking egotist who remained an agreeable character despite his distaste for dogs, children and women. Despite the consistent publicity from his agent and studio, he was in reality a married man who supported his children and grandchildren lovingly.

Fields died at Las Encinas Sanatorium, Pasadena, California; alcohol was an ingredient in the event. His longtime and final love, Carlotta Monti, reported that she went outside and turned the hose onto the roof to allow Fields to hear the sound of falling rain. According to a documentary on his life, he winked and smiled at a nurse, put a finger to his lips, and died.

Other sources claim that he said, 'God damn the whole friggin' world and everyone in it but you, Carlotta.'

Some authorities claim that his final words were, 'I'd rather be in Philadelphia.' It seems that this was the epitaph that Fields proposed for himself in a 1925 article in *Vanity Fair*.

Errol Flynn, 1909–1959
'I shall return.'

Born in Hobart, Tasmania, Flynn earned a name for himself by taking the sort of roles that Douglas Fairbanks Snr played in the silent movies. He became a hero of Hollywood films of the 1930s and 1940s. He became a naturalised American citizen in 1942 so was eligible for the draft. To his own dismay, he failed to join any of the services because he was not physically fit enough.

In October 1959 he was in Vancouver to arrange the lease of his yacht to a wealthy associate. He fell ill and was taken to the flat of a doctor where, despite his condition, a party developed. After some time, he felt even worse, so retired to a bedroom to rest, saying, 'I shall return.' Half an hour later, a friend went to check on him and found him unconscious. He had had a heart attack.

Many publications claim that his final words were, 'I've had a hell of a lot of fun and I've enjoyed every minute of it.' He may well have said them at some point before he died, but they are unlikely to have been his final words.

Charles Frohman, 1856–1915
'Why fear death? It is the most beautiful adventure that life gives us.'

American producer from Ohio. He was on his annual trip to Europe in 1915 when his ship, the *Lusitania*, was torpedoed. Frohman reacted calmly; he stood on the deck smoking a cigar and said, 'This is going to be a close call.' He had a disabled leg and walked with a cane. He knew that he could not jump from the deck into a lifeboat. Instead, he and Alfred Vanderbilt tied lifejackets to 'Moses baskets' containing children who had been in the nursery when the torpedo struck. Frohman then went out onto the deck, where he was joined by three others. In the final moments, they clasped hands and Frohman paraphrased his greatest hit, *Peter Pan*: 'Why fear death? It is the most beautiful adventure that life gives us.' Only one of his party survived. She was standing with Frohman as the ship sank and reported the detail.

Alternative sources report that he said, 'Why fear death? It is the most beautiful adventure in life.'

Charley Goldman, 1887–1968
'Only suckers get hit with right hands.'

Famous American boxer turned manager who trained five world champions, including the undefeated heavyweight Rocky Marciano. He was a colourful character, much enjoyed by sports writers, who fastened on his sharp one-liners. The final words he is alleged to have said probably had more to do with his acknowledged stance on training: 'Only suckers get hit with right hands.'

Edmund Gwenn, 1879–1959
'But it is harder to do comedy.'

English theatre and film actor. He died from pneumonia after having had a stroke, in Woodland Hills, California, twenty days before his eighty-second birthday. The subsequent pneumonia killed him. According to several sources, his last words, when a friend at his bedside remarked, 'It is hard to die,' were, 'But it is harder to do comedy.' A very similar deathbed saying was earlier attributed to the nineteenth-century English actor Edmund Kean, so the association of the words with Gwenn may be misplaced.

Richard Harris, 1930–2002
'It was the food; don't touch the food!'

An Irish actor from Limerick, he appeared on stage and in many films. *Camelot* was one of his great successes. He also played Albus Dumbledore in the first two films in the Harry Potter series.

Harris was a man who lived life to the full. He drank prodigiously until he gave up booze for ten years from 1981. He was diagnosed with Hodgkin's disease in August 2002, reportedly after being hospitalised with pneumonia.

Some claim that he was taken ill while dining in a hotel in London. As he was wheeled out on a stretcher he said, 'It was the food; don't touch the food!' The truth is that he was in a coma for the final three days of his life and nobody recorded his final words.

Jon Erik Hexum, 1957–1984
'Let's see if this will do it.'

American television actor with a hugely muscled body which gave him a modelling career too.

Hexum was playing a character in a series called *Golden Opportunity* in October 1984. The part required him to load blanks into a .44 Magnum handgun. The scene did not work as the director wanted and while the crew sorted out his orders, Hexum toyed with the weapon, from which he had unloaded all but one blank round. He then said, 'Let's see if this will do it,' put the revolver to his head and pulled the trigger. He didn't die immediately, but was pronounced brain-dead six days later.

Alfred Hitchcock, 1899–1980
'One has to die to know exactly what happens after death, although Catholics have their hopes.'

English film director and producer. His métier was suspense and he is credited with pioneering many techniques to improve his films. He loved to appear, if only briefly, in his own films. He moved to Hollywood in 1939 and became a US citizen in 1955.

Hitchcock died of renal failure in his home on 29 April 1980. Two Jesuit priests performed Mass and heard his Confession.

Some say that his final words were, 'One never knows the ending. One has to die to know exactly what happens after death, although Catholics have their hopes.' But in view of the known circumstances of his death, this quote seems to have more to do with his stance on film making.

Bob Hope, 1903–2003
'Surprise me.'

English-born American comedian, actor, singer, dancer, author and athlete who enjoyed a glittering career over sixty years. He was a very funny man who delivered the most brilliant one-liners. It was said that his timing was the key.

Hope maintained his self-deprecating sense of humour, quipping when he was ninety-five, 'I'm so old, they've cancelled my blood type.' He died at his home in Toluca Lake, Los Angeles two months after his 100th birthday. His grandson Zach Hope reported that when asked on his deathbed where he wanted to be buried, Hope told his wife, 'Surprise me.'

Al Jolson, 1886–1950
'Boys, I'm going.'

An adoptive American singer, comedian, and actor from modern-day Lithuania. He particularly enjoyed performing in blackface makeup and often played the part of a black manservant who was always more clever than his masters.

Early in 1950 he volunteered to go to Korea to entertain the troops. After a long pause, the Secretary of Defense responded that they didn't have enough money to pay for entertainment. Jolson interpreted the message as an assault on his sense of patriotism. 'What are they talkin' about?' he thundered. 'Funds? Who needs funds? I got funds! I'll pay myself!'

He duly travelled to Korea and achieved his objective, doing forty-two shows in sixteen days. He returned home but the dust of Korea had settled in his only surviving lung and he was close to exhaustion. While playing cards in his suite at the St Francis Hotel in San Francisco, Jolson collapsed and died of a massive heart attack on 23 October 1950. His last words were said to be, 'Boys, I'm going.' He was sixty-four.

Groucho Marx, 1890–1977
'Don't be silly. Everybody has a temperature.'

An American comedian and film and television star whose real name was Julius Henry Marx. He was the youngest of three siblings, who made a number of feature films as the Marx Brothers. His style was to affect a stoop, smoke a cigar and wear a thick fake moustache and eyebrows. He was admired for his rapid wit. He married and divorced three times.

Marx developed pneumonia and was admitted to hospital on 22 June 1977. He died on 19 August at Cedars Sinai Medical Center in Los Angeles. While he was in hospital on his deathbed, a nurse came around with a thermometer, explaining that she wanted to see if he had a temperature. He responded, 'Don't be silly – everybody has a temperature.'

Leonard 'Chico' Marx, 1887–1961
'Put in my coffin a deck of cards, a mashie niblick and a pretty blonde.'

An American comedian and actor from New York. The oldest of the Marx Brothers, he was always cast as the dim-witted but crafty conman. He wore shabby clothes, and sported a curly-haired wig and Tyrolean hat.

Chico Marx died of hardening of the arteries on 11 October 1961 at his Hollywood home. He is reported to have said, 'Remember, Honey, don't forget what I told you. Put in my coffin a deck of cards, a mashie niblick and a pretty blonde.'

Louis B. Mayer, 1884–1957
'Nothing matters. Nothing matters.'

Born in Minsk, Russia, he emigrated to the USA and became a prolific film producer. As the studio boss of MGM, which he achieved through devious means, he built the business into a financially successful model.

Louis B. Mayer died of leukaemia on 29 October 1957. His last words were reported as, 'Nothing matters. Nothing matters.'

Vic Morrow, 1929–1982
'I should have asked for a stunt double.'

American actor who played in a range of television and film shows. He and two children were on set filming *Twilight Zone: The Movie* when a helicopter that was trying to perform a stunt crashed, killing the three of them. Just before the scene started, he said, 'I should have asked for a stunt double.'

Lawrence Olivier, 1907–1989
'This isn't *Hamlet*, you know. It's not meant to go in the bloody ear.'
A British actor, director, and producer. He was, perhaps, one of the most famous and revered actors of the twentieth century and the first to be elevated to the peerage. He was married three times, to the actresses Jill Esmond, Vivien Leigh, and Joan Plowright.

His friend Gawn Grainger reported that he was not present at Olivier's death but had heard that a nurse had spilled some juice in the great man's ear, evoking the final words, 'This isn't *Hamlet*, you know. It's not meant to go in the bloody ear.'

Anna Pavlova, 1881–1931
'Play the last measure very softly.'
Russian Empire ballerina born in St Petersburg, the illegitimate child of a laundress and, some say, a banker. She is widely regarded as one of the finest classical ballet dancers in history.

Pavlova learned that she had pneumonia when she was on tour in The Hague and was told that the surgeons would have to operate. The trouble was that they warned that she would never be able to dance again. She refused to have the surgery, saying, 'If I can't dance then I'd rather be dead.' In the event, she died of pleurisy. There are two stories of her final words. In one, she was holding her costume from *The Dying Swan* and said, 'Play the last measure very softly.'

Some sources claim that her final words were, 'Get my swan costume ready.'

Freddie Prinze, 1954–1977
'Nobody had anything to do with this. My decision totally.'
An American actor and stand-up comedian. He married very young and was divorced fifteen months later. In the weeks following his divorce, Prinze began to suffer from depression and this was not helped by a difficult conversation with his estranged wife on the night of 28 January 1977. A little later, his business manager, Marvin 'Dusty' Snyder arrived. He witnessed Prinze put a gun to his head and shoot himself. He had left a note, which read, 'I must end it. There's no hope left. I'll be at peace. No one had anything to do with this. My decision totally.'

Will Rogers, 1879 – 1935
'Well, Wiley's got her warmed up. Let's go.'

An American cowboy and actor from Oklahoma. He was one of the world's best-known celebrities in the 1920s and 1930s. In 1928 he mounted a fake campaign for the presidency, promising only that if he were elected, he would resign. Many of his other quick-fire jokes reveal a caustic but clear-eyed humour ('I belong to no organised party. I'm a Democrat.').

In 1935 Wiley Post, another Oklahoman, was interested in surveying a mail-and-passenger air route from the West Coast to Russia. Rogers visited Post often at the airport in Burbank, California, while he was modifying his aircraft for water landings and eventually asked Post to fly him through Alaska to research new material for his newspaper column.

On 15 August, they left Fairbanks, Alaska, for Point Barrow. They were a few miles from their destination when they landed in a lagoon to ask for directions. As they prepared to take off, Rogers broadcast the words, 'Well, Wiley's got her warmed up. Let's go.'

As they took off, the engine failed at low altitude. There was no way to recover and they plunged into the water, shearing off the right wing and ending up inverted in the shallow water of the lagoon. Both men died instantly.

George Sanders, 1906–1972
'I am leaving you with your worries in this sweet cesspool. Good luck.'

Sanders was a British actor, singer-songwriter and composer. Born in Saint Petersburg, he always had a 'heavy' accent, which lent itself to roles as a villain.

Sanders had dementia and was unsteady on his feet. He had a minor stroke and, concerned at the loss of health, he became deeply depressed. After selling his house in Majorca, he drifted from place to place. Eventually he came to earth in a coastal town near Barcelona in April 1972 and was found dead two days later. He had taken a great deal of barbiturates. He left behind three suicide notes, which all read, 'Dear World, I am leaving because I am bored. I feel I have lived long enough. I am leaving you with your worries in this sweet cesspool. Good luck.'

Rudolf Valentino, 1895–1926
'Don't worry, chief. It will be alright.'

An Italian actor of the silent movie era who became a sex symbol. His arrival in New York in 1913 was the start of four hard years, during which he worked wherever he could to earn money. His luck started to turn after becoming a dancer at Maxim's.

In August 1926, Valentino collapsed at the Hotel Ambassador in New York. He needed an immediate operation to deal with his appendix and gastric ulcers. Things did not go well and he developed peritonitis. His doctors were unwisely optimistic because he was then diagnosed with severe pleuritis (which is extreme inflammation to the lungs and is very painful). Abruptly the doctors realised that he was going to die but decided not to tell the actor, who believed that his condition would improve. Shortly before he fell into a coma, he said, 'Don't worry, chief. It will be alright'

Karl Wallenda, 1905–1978
'Hold tight.'

A German-American high-wire artist from Magdeburg in Germany. He established a daredevil circus act which performed dangerous activities like a skywalk across the Tallulah Gorge in Georgia. More often than not he worked without a safety net.

At the age of seventy-three, Wallenda attempted a walk between the two towers of the ten-story Condado Plaza Hotel in San Juan. The wire was 37 metres above the pavement, there was no safety net and the wiring support was faulty. The exercise was further bedevilled by high winds. He fell to his death and the whole thing was captured on film by a crew from the local television station. Some say that, as he mounted the wire, his final words were, 'Hold tight.'

John Wayne, 1907–1979
'Did you see that flash of light?'

American film actor, producer and director who focused on Wild West movies. His real name was Marion Robert Morrison and he was born in Iowa.

The name Marion never seems to have been an impediment, but as a boy he used to go around with his dog, Duke. People started to call him 'Little Duke', which he preferred to his given name. The 'little' was soon dropped and he was commonly known as 'Duke' for the remainder of his life.

He survived a bout of lung cancer in 1964 but died of stomach cancer in 1979 at the UCLA Medical Center in Los Angeles. It seems that ninety-one people who took part in the 1956 *film The Conqueror* on location near St George, Utah, subsequently presented symptoms of cancer and people attributed this to the proximity of the location to a government nuclear testing station in Nevada. But Wayne believed that his lung cancer derived from the six packs of cigarettes he smoked every day. His last words were, 'Did you see that flash of light?'

James Whale, 1889–1957
'I must have peace and this is the only way.'

Film director noted for his horror movies, which included *Frankenstein* (1931), *The Old Dark House* (1932), *The Invisible Man* (1933) and *Bride of Frankenstein* (1935). He served in the Army during the Second World War and was a prisoner of war. Curiously this allowed him to develop his interest in drama, so he turned to the theatre. After a successful production of *Journey's End* in London, he directed it on Broadway before moving on to Hollywood, where he spent the remainder of his life.

He committed suicide by drowning himself in his swimming pool, leaving a note which was suppressed by his live-in lover, David Lewis. For decades it was thought that his death was accidental, but Lewis released it shortly before his own death. It read, 'To ALL I LOVE, Do not grieve for me. My nerves are all shot and for the last year I have been in agony day and night – except when I sleep with sleeping pills – and any peace I have by day is when I am drugged by pills. I have had a wonderful life but it is over and my nerves get worse and I am afraid they will have to take me away. So please forgive me, all those I love and may God forgive me too, but I cannot bear the agony and it is best for everyone this way. The future is just old age and illness and pain. Goodbye and thank you for all your love. I must have peace and this is the only way.'

Florenz Ziegfeld, 1867–1932
'The show looks good. The show looks good.'

American Broadway impresario born in Chicago who made a small fortune and lost most of it in the financial crash of 1932. He died of pleurisy in California and his final words were recorded as, 'Curtain! Fast music! Light! Ready for the last finale! Great! The show looks good. The show looks good.'

Businessmen and Philanthropists

Andrew Bradford, 1686–1742
'Oh Lord, forgive the misprints.'

Born in Philadelphia, he followed his father's lead and became a printer in Philadelphia. One of his claims to fame is that he employed Benjamin Franklin, who subsequently started a rival printing business. His final words are probably apocryphal: 'O Lord, forgive the misprints.'

Conrad Hilton, 1887–1979
'Leave the shower curtain on the inside of the tub.'

Born in San Antonio, he was the son of a Norwegian immigrant father and Catholic German American mother. His philanthropy was drawn from the influence of his family and the Catholic Church. Founder of the Hilton hotel empire, he bought his first hotel in Texas in 1919. One report suggests that rooms changed hands up to three times a day, which indicates something more than pure hotel activity. He narrowly avoided bankruptcy during the Great Depression, but fought back and eventually regained control of his business. Much of his fortune was left to a charitable foundation, the Conrad N. Hilton Foundation, which he established in 1944. Allegedly, when asked if he had any last words of wisdom, he replied, 'Leave the shower curtain on the inside of the tub.'

Steve Jobs, 1955–2011
'Oh wow, oh wow, oh wow.'

The American entrepreneur and inventor was born in San Fransisco. He co-founded Apple Inc. with Steve Wozniak and Ronald Wayne in 1976. There was a falling out in 1985 and Jobs left the business to set up NEXT. In 1996 he returned to Apple, which was close to going out of business. As interim CEO he turned the business around and cemented his place as the permanent CEO and Chairman of Apple. Famously he drew a salary of just $1 per year from the company, although his 5,426 million shares in the business gave him a good return and were worth $2.1 billion. His 138 million shares in Disney were worth $4.4 billion.

He was diagnosed with pancreatic cancer in 2003, and it eventually killed him. He sank into a coma the day before he died in the presence of his wife and children. His sister recorded that his last words were, 'Oh wow, oh wow, oh wow.'

John Pierpont Morgan, 1837–1913
'I've got to get to the top of the hill.'

An American financier born in Hartford, Connecticut. He proved to be brilliant at mergers and acquisitions. He was a big man, both in size and personality, although he had a deformed nose which made him relatively ugly.

He died in Rome in his sleep at the age of seventy-five, leaving his fortune and business to his son, John Pierpont 'Jack' Morgan Jr, and left his mansion and large book collections to the Morgan Library & Museum in New York.

Several sources claim that his final words were, 'I've got to get to the top of the hill,' but it is most unlikely since nobody thought to record his words as he went to bed.

Lord Northcliffe, 1865–1922
'Take that.'

Alfred Harmsworth was born in Chapelizod, County Dublin on 15 July 1865. He started his newspaper career by producing the school magazine at Stamford in Lincolnshire. His first commercial venture was the launch of *Answers to Correspondents* before buying a number of failing newspapers. He became a great press baron, owner of the *Daily Mail*, the *Daily Mirror*, the *Observer*, *The Times* and *The Sunday Times*.

He died of heart disease in a hut on the roof of his London house, No. 1 Carlton House Gardens, in August 1922. He is said to have pulled a gun from beneath his pillow and pointed it at an irritating visitor. 'Take that,' he said, and died. Happily, the weapon had no bullets because his valet had removed them.

He left three months' pay to each of his 6,000 employees.

Cecil John Rhodes, 1853–1902
'So little done. So much to do.'

Born in Bishop's Stortford, the fifth son of a priest whose claim to fame was that he never preached a sermon that lasted longer than ten minutes. Rhodes was a sickly child so his father decided to send him abroad to stay with his uncle in Natal.

In 1871 Rhodes and his brother moved to Kimberley, and over the course of some seventeen years he bought up small diamond mining businesses, thereby creating De Beers. In his will, he established the famous Rhodes Scholarship, the world's first international study program. The objective was to promote leadership.

He experienced ill health from an early age and died of heart failure at the age of forty-eight. It is possible that his death was hastened by the mischievous claim of Princess Catherine Radziwill, who asked him to marry her. He declined, so she accused him of fraud and the case went to trial. He died a short time later. Many sources claim that his last words were, 'So little done. So much to do,' but this is probably a myth.

Criminals and Revolutionaries

Jesus Ledesma Aguilar, 1963–2006
'Are you happy I'm dying?'

Born in Venezuela, Aguilar became a professional baseball player with the Cleveland Indians.

Aguilar went off the rails and became involved in the drugs scene. In company with another he shot Leonardo Chavez and his wife Annette. They were seen by the couple's nine-year-old son, who identified Aguilar in a newspaper picture. Aguilar had already spent time in prison for shooting a policeman, so he was given the death sentence, while his partner in crime merely received a life sentence.

He spoke as the lethal dose began to flow. 'I would like to say to my family, I am all right.' He then tried to find Leonardo Chavez Jr, who had witnessed the shooting of his parents eleven years earlier. 'Where are you, Leo? Are you there, Leo? Don't lie, man.' And finally he said, 'Are you happy I'm dying?'

James Allen (Red Dog), 1954–1993
'The rest of you can kiss my ass.'

A Sioux Indian who was in and out of jail throughout his whole life. Many judged that he should not have been released after an earlier conviction and sentence for murder. He was finally caught and sentenced for the brutal rape of a neighbour (eighty years) and the murder of her housemate (death by lethal injection). His last words were, 'The rest of you can kiss my ass.'

George Appel, ?–1928
'You are about to see a baked Appel.'

Appel murdered a police officer in New York in 1928. He was captured, tried and sentenced to death. As they strapped him into the electric chair, he said to his executioners 'Well, gentlemen, you are about to see a baked Appel.'

Sam Bass, 1851–1878
'Let me go – the world is bobbing around me.'

Bass turned to crime after failing to make his way in legitimate business. He formed a gang and held up the Union Pacific gold train from San Fransisco, escaping with the then massive amount of $60,000. Bass managed to elude arrest until one of his gang turned informant. The gang planned to rob the Williamson Bank in Round Rock, Texas. An ambush was laid and when some of the gang were scouting the site, Deputy Sheriff A. W. Grimes approached them and was shot dead. Bass attempted to get away, and was shot by two Rangers. He was found lying in a pasture by a group of railroad workers. He was taken into custody and died the next day, his twenty-seventh birthday. His last words were, 'Let me go – the world is bobbing around me.'

William Boyd, 4th Earl of Kilmarnock, 1704–1746
'I beg you'll get my wife, or my successors to pay them when they can ... '

Kilmarnock decided to join the cause of the Young Pretender, Charles Edward Stuart, in the rebellion of 1745. He became a Privy Counsellor, and was eventually a general. He fought at Falkirk and Culloden, where he was taken prisoner. Transported to London, he was tried and then beheaded on Tower Hill on 18 August 1746 in company with Arthur Elphinstone.

Before his execution in August 1746, he wrote to a friend from prison about his debt to the shoemakers of Elgin, explaining that he had ordered some seventy pairs of shoes for his men but had failed to pay them. At the end of a long letter, he wrote, 'If you'll write to Mr Innes of Dalkinty at Elgin (with whom I was quartered when I lay there), he will send you an account of the shoes, and if they were paid to the shoemakers or no; and if they are not, I beg you'll get my wife, or my successors to pay them when they can ... '

John Brown, 1800–1859
'I am ready at any time. Do not keep me waiting.'

An abolitionist from Torrington, Connecticut, who used militant actions to abolish slavery in the United States. The song 'John Brown's Body' made him a heroic martyr and was a popular Union marching song during the Civil War. Brown and his men attacked the Harper's Ferry Armoury on 16 February 1859. By the 18th the US Marines, under command of Colonel Robert E. Lee, surrounded the engine house, which became known as John Brown's Fort. The

Marines were too powerful and offered to spare the lives of the rebels provided they gave up. They declined and John Brown was subsequently hanged. He said to his executioners, 'I am ready at any time. Do not keep me waiting.'

Robert Catesby, 1573–1603
'Stand by me, Tom. We will die together.'

The leader of the Gunpowder Plot. After Guy Fawkes was found guarding the barrels, Catesby made a stand at Holbeche House in Staffordshire, against a 200-strong company of armed men led by the Sheriff of Worcester. He was shot, and was later found dead, clutching a picture of the Virgin Mary. Tom Wintour, another of the conspirators, was with him and was shot dead. This lends some credibility to the alleged final words, 'Stand by me, Tom. We will die together,' but no one survived to validate them.

Arthur Elphinstone, 6th Lord Balmerino, 1675–1746
'My Lord, I wish I could suffer for both.'

He joined the Jacobite cause in the uprising of 1715. He escaped after the battle of Sherrifmuir and fled to France, where he joined the French Army. His father managed to obtain a pardon for him so that he could return home, but he was unrepentant and was captured at the Battle of Culloden. At his execution at the Tower of London, he and his fellow Jacobite, Lord Kilmarnock, embraced and Balmerino is reported to have said, 'My Lord, I wish I could suffer for both.'

Bernard Coy, 1901–1946
'It don't matter; I figure I licked the Rock anyway.'

A native of Kentucky who turned to crime during the Depression. He became an unsuccessful bank robber and was sentenced to twenty-five years in prison. After a spell in Atlanta, he was transferred to Alcatraz in May 1946. Here he enjoyed a degree of freedom as an orderly, which gave him the idea that he could break into the gun gallery, steal some weapons and make an escape. It turned into a bloody two-day armed confrontation. The escapees seized some guards and there was a prolonged standoff. History does not properly record the sequence of events after that, but Coy and his two fellow inmates were found dead. Before he died, he is alleged to have said, 'It don't matter; I figure I licked the Rock anyway.'

Francis 'Two Gun' Crowley, 1912–1932
'You sons of bitches. Give my love to Mother.'

An American career criminal from New York, who was captured after a major shoot-out with the 300 New York Police sent to capture him. Apparently 15,000 spectators witnessed the two-hour event. To his executioners, as they were tying him into the electric chair, he said ,'You sons of bitches. Give my love to Mother.'

Bennie Demps, 1951–2000
'This is not an execution, it is murder.'

Demps was sentenced to death for three murders overall and, in each case, the evidence was sketchy and unreliable. Indeed, one of the reasons the judge meted out the death sentence for the third murder (of a co-prisoner in jail) was because of the two earlier murders for which he was being held. A review of the last case showed that the conviction was wholly unreliable.

Florida demands that executioners use two separate intravenous injections onto different veins. On this occasion the medical team could only find one and it took thirty-three minutes to fail to find the second one. They gave up.

His last words were, 'They butchered me back there, I was in a lot of pain. They cut me in the groin; they cut me in the leg. I was bleeding profusely. This is not an execution, it is murder.'

Robert Drew, 1959–1994
'Remember, the death penalty is murder.'

Although not entirely innocent of any crime, Drew proved to be the victim of a gross miscarriage of justice when he was convicted of the murder of one Jeffrey Mays on the exclusive evidence of the actual killer. In a plea bargain which converted his probable death sentence into a sixty-year prison sentence, Ernest Purleauski swore that Drew had stabbed Mays. Years later he recanted his testimony saying that he alone was responsible for the murder. Drew's final statement was carefully prepared and included more than the commonly quoted, 'Remember, the death penalty is murder.'

Georg Engel, 1836–1887
'Hurra für die Anarchie! Dies ist der glücklichste Moment meines Lebens.'

One of the four people executed for the 1886 Haymarket bombing in Chicago. Curiously, he was playing cards at home when the bombing was carried out, but he was arrested, tried and sentence to death. He wrote to the governor to say that he did not want any clemency. As he arrived at the gallows, he shouted in his native German, 'Hurra für die Anarchie! Dies ist der glücklichste Moment meines Lebens.' ('Hurrah for anarchy! This is the happiest moment of my life.')

Earl Ferrers, 1720–1760
'Am I right?'

Laurence Shirley, 4th Earl Ferrers, was the last peer of the realm to be executed as a felon.

Ferrers was not in charge of the family estate, which was managed by trustees. They appointed a man called Johnson as the receiver of rents. He performed honestly and diligently and was not inclined to do what the earl asked of him. In January 1760, Johnson called at Staunton Harold in Leicestershire by appointment and was taken to see the earl in his study. After a brief conversation, Lord Ferrers shot and killed Johnson. Ferrers was tried for murder by his peers in Westminster Hall. His defence, which he conducted in person, was a plea of insanity. Although there was some supporting evidence, he was found guilty of the murder.

He is said to have announced that one should look one's best for one's execution, so he wore his wedding suit. A new gallows was constructed at Tyburn and the crowds were so great that it took almost three hours to travel from the Tower of London to the gallows. Here his arms were tied with a black silk sash, and the rope placed around his neck. His final words were to ask Turlis, his executioner, 'Am I right?' A white nightcap, which Ferrers had brought with him, was pulled down over his head and the hangman let him drop.

Hans Frank, 1900–1946
'Ich bitte Gott, mich mit Gnade zu akzeptieren.'

Frank was a German lawyer from Karlsruhe who worked for the Nazi party during the 1920s and 1930s. He was elected to the Reichstag in 1930 and was appointed Minister of Justice for Bavaria in 1933. In 1939 he became Governor General of the occupied Polish territory and initiated a reign of terror against the civilian population. He was an active participant in the mass murder of Polish Jews. At the Nuremberg trials, he was found guilty of war crimes and crimes against humanity. He was sentenced to be executed.

Frank was one of just two war criminals to express remorse for their actions. On being led to the execution chamber, he is reported to have said, 'My conscience does not allow me simply to throw the responsibility solely on minor people ... A thousand years will pass and still Germany's guilt will not have been erased.' When asked for any last statement, he replied, 'I am thankful for the kind treatment during my captivity and I ask God to accept me with mercy.'

James French, 1936–1966
'How about this for a headline for tomorrow's paper? French fries!'

An American criminal, who kidnapped a man who gave him a lift as he hitch-hiked across Texas in 1958. Sentenced to life in prison, he murdered a fellow prisoner in 1961 and was sentenced to die. He was the only prisoner executed in the United States in 1966.

As they strapped him into the electric chair, he said, 'How about this for a headline for tomorrow's paper? French fries!'

Johnny Frank Garrett Snr, 1963–1992
'And the rest of the world can kiss my ass.'

Executed for the rape and murder of a seventy-six-year-old nun in 1981, subsequent DNA evidence strongly suggests that he was not guilty of the crime, which seems to have been committed by one Leoncio Perez Rueda. Garrett was severely mentally handicapped and that alone put the entire case into question. The state of Texas came under heavy criticism for allowing both a juvenile and mentally handicapped individual to be executed.

His final words were alleged to be, 'I'd like to thank my family for loving me and taking care of me. And the rest of the world can kiss my ass,' which is pretty much what James Allen (Red Dog) said.

Jimmy L. Glass, 1962–1987
'I'd rather be fishing.'

Glass had a criminal record before raising the stakes by killing people. He and another man, Jimmy Wingo, escaped from Webster Parish Jail in December 1982. On a rampage, they attempted to burgle the home of Newton and Erline Brown, and shot them dead. Glass was soon arrested, tried and sentenced to death in the electric chair.

He made headlines in 1985 when he appealed to the Supreme Court, arguing that executions by electrocution violated the Eighth and Fourteenth Amendments to the United States Constitution. But the Court, by a majority of five to four, found that electrocution was constitutional.

Glass was electrocuted on 12 June 1987 at the age of twenty-five. Governor Edwin W. Edwards refused to commute the sentence. His last words are alleged to have been, 'I'd rather be fishing.'

Barbara Graham, 1923–1955
'Good people are always so sure they're right.'

Something of a social misfit, Graham was born Barbara Elaine Wood in Oakland, California. Her mother was sent to reform school when Barbara was just two years old, so she was brought up by strangers and extended family. In due course she had to serve a sentence in the same reform school where her mother had been.

She married the hardened criminal and drug addict Henry Graham. She had an affair with one of Graham's criminal associates, Emmett Perkins, with whom she and others decided to burgle the home of an elderly woman, Mabel Monohan, who was alleged to have a large amount of cash in the house. The gang assaulted Ms Monohan as soon as she opened her front door and, despite their worst efforts, she resolutely resisted their attempts to force her to tell them where her valuables were. Barbara Graham is said to have cracked her skull with a pistol before they smothered her.

One of the gang members testified against the rest in exchange for immunity from prosecution. Graham was found guilty and sentenced to execution in the gas chamber. She asked for a blindfold and her final words were, 'Good people are always so sure they're right.'

Thomas J. Grasso, 1962–1995
'I did not get my Spaghetti-O's. I got spaghetti. I want the Press to know this.'

Grasso committed two murders, one in Oklahoma and one in New York. He was caught and put on trial in New York, but a legal argument ensued when Oklahoma laid claim to the right to execute him. In due course, he was executed by lethal injection at Oklahoma State Penitentiary on 20 March 1995, for the murder of eighty-seven-year-old Hilda Johnson in Tulsa, Oklahoma, and eighty-one-year-old Leslie Holtz in Staten Island, New York. He was active in persuading the authorities not to delay his execution with endless appeals, so went through the system in sixty days. When asked about his last meal, he said, 'I did not get my Spaghetti-O's. I got spaghetti. I want the Press to know this.'

G.W. Green, 1936–1991
'Lock and load. Let's do it. Ain't life a … [expletive deleted]'

Green was one of three men who broke into a house in Montgomery County, Texas, in 1976 to steal the gun collection of the owner, who was a juvenile probation officer and deputy sheriff. Green did not fire the weapon that killed the house owner, John Denson, but he never showed any remorse and is alleged to have encouraged the gunman to shoot the victim's wife and child. After fifteen years of appeals, the execution was finally confirmed.

His final words were, 'Lock and load. Let's do it. Ain't life a ….[expletive deleted].' He died by lethal injection.

Ernesto 'Che' Guevara, 1928–1967
'Sé que usted ha venido a matarme. Dispara cobarde, sólo vas a matar a un hombre.'

Che was an Argentine revolutionary. As a young medical student, he experienced the intense poverty of South America, which persuaded him that he should join in action to bring social reform. His life was changed when he met Fidel and Raul Castro in Mexico and elected to join them in taking Cuba. He became a major figure of the Cuban Revolution. Even he must have been surprised by the cult status he achieved.

He was captured by Bolivian special forces after an informer told them of his encampment in the Yuro ravine. He was wounded during the engagement and taken prisoner. Two days later, Bolivian President René Barrientos ordered that Guevara be killed.

The executioner was Mario Terán, a half-drunken sergeant in the Bolivian army who had requested to shoot Guevara. To make the bullet wounds appear consistent with the story the government planned to release to the public, Félix Rodríguez ordered Terán to aim carefully to make it appear that Guevara had been killed in action during a clash with the Bolivian army.

Terán made a hash of the job, shooting Guevara nine times (five in his legs, once in the right shoulder and arm, once in the chest, and finally in the throat). Shortly before he fired, Guevara shouted, 'Sé que usted ha venido a matarme. Dispara cobarde, sólo vas a matar a un hombre.' ('I know you have come to kill me. Do it. Shoot me, you coward, you are only going to kill a man.')

Robert Alton Harris, 1953–1992
'You can be a king or a street sweeper, but everyone dances with the Grim Reaper.'

He murdered two boys in San Diego in 1978. After a series of appeals, his execution was the first in California since 1967. His final words were, 'You can be a king or a street sweeper, but everyone dances with the Grim Reaper.'

Leonel Herrera, 1947–1993
'May God bless you all. I am ready.'

He was sentenced to death for murdering two Texas police officers on 29 September 1981 at separate locations along a highway between Brownsville and Los Fresnos. It seems entirely possible that he was innocent, taking the blame for the actions of his brother. His conviction was cemented by the presence of his social security card at the scene of one of the murders and the identification of his car as the one used by the murderer.

Information about his innocence and his brother's guilt was produced, but the US Supreme Court would not overturn the judgement.

His statement before his execution by lethal injection was, 'I am innocent, innocent, innocent. Make no mistake about this; I owe society nothing. Continue the struggle for human rights, helping those who are innocent, especially Mr Graham. I am an innocent man, and something very wrong is taking place tonight. May God bless you all. I am ready.'

Joe Hill (also known as Joel Emmanuel Hagglund or Joseph Hillstrom), 1879-1915
'Fire.'

A Swedish American labour activist and singer. His most famous songs include 'The Preacher and the Slave', 'The Tramp', 'There is Power in a Union', 'The Rebel Girl' and 'Casey Jones – the Union Scab'. His very last word was 'Fire!'

In 1914, John G. Morrison, a Salt Lake City grocer and former policeman, and his son were killed by two men. That evening, Hill arrived at a doctor's office with a gunshot wound, and briefly mentioned a fight over a woman. He was later accused of the grocery store murders on the basis of his injury and was convicted in a controversial trial. It is likely that he wasn't guilty of the crime for which he was executed because evidence found after his execution proved that his injury was caused in a private fight with his love rival.

His last will, which was eventually set to music by Ethel Raim, founder of the group the Pennywhistlers, reads,

My will is easy to decide,
For there is nothing to divide.
My kin don't need to fuss and moan,
'Moss does not cling to a rolling stone.'

My body? Oh, if I could choose
I would to ashes it reduce,
And let the merry breezes blow,
My dust to where some flowers grow.

Perhaps some fading flower then
Would come to life and bloom again.
This is my Last and final Will.
Good Luck to all of you.

He was executed by firing squad and interrupted the deputy's orders, 'Ready … Aim,' by shouting, 'Fire!'

Jesse James, 1847–1882
'This picture is awful dusty.'

James, who was born in Kearney, Missouri, was an American gang leader who robbed banks and trains, committing murder at will. He was the most famous member of the James–Younger Gang.

Over time the quality of the gang deteriorated and James moved around America, turning up in Missouri, Alabama, Louisiana and Tennessee. He came to trust only Charley and Robert Ford. What James did not know was that Robert had been dealing secretly with the Missouri governor to bring the outlaw to justice.

On 3 April 1882, after breakfast, the Fords and James prepared to depart for another robbery. As he was leaving the house, he noticed a dusty picture on the wall and stood on a chair to clean it, saying, 'This picture is awful dusty.' Robert Ford then shot James in the back of the head.

The Ford brothers were pleased with their action and didn't resist arrest. Indeed, Robert sent a message to the governor to claim his reward. In a single day they were tried, sentenced to death and given a full pardon by the governor.

Ned Kelly, 1855–1880
'Ah well, I suppose it has to come to this. Such is life.'

An Irish Australian born in Beveridge, Victoria, he was often in trouble with the police but he was not perceived as a major threat until an incident at his home in 1878. A major hunt out in the bush tried to track him down, during which he killed three policemen.

He was captured after a violent stand-off at Glenrowan on 28 June 1880. Kelly had created a home-made metal suit of armour and a helmet. He was captured and convicted of three counts of capital murder. He was hanged at Old Melbourne Gaol in November 1880. Some still see him as a folk hero.

On the scaffold on 11 November 1880 he said, 'Ah well, I suppose it has to come to this. Such is life.'

Madame du Barry, 1743–1793
'Juste un instant, je vous prie!'

Jeanne Bécu was born at Vaucouleurs, in Lorraine, the illegitimate daughter of Anne Bécu, a woman of extraordinary beauty. Jeanne inherited her mother's beauty and came to the attention of a high-class pimp nicknamed 'Le roué.' This was Jean-Baptiste du Barry, who gave her the name Mademoiselle Lange. She quickly acquired a reputation in Paris, with many lovers who were aristocratic or close to the monarchy. She was presented at court in April 1769 and in very little time became the mistress of Louis XV.

After the death of the king, she was exiled to the Abbey du Pont-aux-Dames near Meaux-en-Brie, where she was kept under close supervision for a year. At the end of that time, she was given most of the freedom she needed, although she was not allowed to go near Versailles.

In 1793 the Revolutionary Tribunal of Paris accused her of treason. She was condemned to death. On 8 December she was beheaded by the guillotine in the Place de la Révolution.

As she was being taken to the scaffold she shouted, 'Vous allez me faire du mal. S'il vous plaît ne pas me faire de mal, juste un instant, je vous prie!' ('You are going to hurt me. Please don't hurt me, just one more moment, I beg you!')

James Duke of Monmouth, 1649–1685
'Do not hack me as you did my lord Russell.'

An English nobleman born in Rotterdam. Originally called James Crofts or James Fitzroy, he was the eldest illegitimate son of Charles II of England and his mistress, Lucy Walter. He became the 1st Duke of Monmouth and the 1st Duke of Buccleuch. He served in the Second Anglo-Dutch War and commanded British troops taking part in the Third Anglo-Dutch War before commanding the Anglo-Dutch brigade fighting in the Franco-Dutch War. Monmouth was executed by beheading in 1685 after making an unsuccessful attempt to depose his uncle, King James II. This was the Monmouth Rebellion. His last words, quoted by T.B. Macaulay in his *History of England*, Volume 1 (1849), were, 'Do not hack me as you did my Lord Russell.'

Mario Benjamin Murphy, 1972–1997
'Today is a good day to die. I forgive all of you. I hope God does too.'

A professional hitman, Murphy was a Mexican who was hired by the wife of the victim. He was paid $5,000, and the wife and her boyfriend hoped to collect $100,000 from a life insurance policy. Murphy confessed to carrying out the murder. Murphy recruited other people for the mission and all the others aside from Murphy were given life sentences. Murphy himself was executed by lethal injection in Virginia on 17 September 1997.

His last words were 'Today is a good day to die. I forgive all of you. I hope God does too.'

William Palmer, 1824–1856
'Are you sure this damn thing is safe?'

Known as the Rugeley Poisoner, Palmer was an English doctor convicted for the 1855 murder of his friend John Cook, whom he poisoned with strychnine. He was suspected of poisoning several other people, all of them family. He was completely unscrupulous, killing and defrauding in order to gain money from his victims or their estates. He lost most of it gambling on horses. He was tried at the Old Bailey.

His execution at Stafford prison drew an enormous crowd. As he stepped onto the scaffold, he said to the executioner, 'Are you sure this damn thing is safe?'

Carl Panzram, 1891–1930
'Hurry it up, you Hoosier bastard! I could hang a dozen men while you're screwing around.'

Carl Panzram was a nasty piece of work from Polk County, Minnesota . He started his criminal career as a petty thief, but worked his way up to burglary, arson, rape and murder. He was arrested for burglary in 1928 and owned up to killing two boys. Then, in graphic detail, Panzram confessed to twenty-one murders and to having sodomised over 1,000 males, quite apart from committing thousands of burglaries and other crimes. Surprisingly, he received only a life sentence, but he went on to murder the foreman of the prison laundry and was tried and sentenced to hang. As the noose was put around his neck, he said, 'Hurry it up, you Hoosier bastard! I could hang a dozen men while you're screwing around.'

73

James W. Rodgers, 1910–1960
'I done told you my last request – a bulletproof vest.'

An American from Lubbock, Texas, whose rough childhood certainly contributed to his career as an armed robber. He spent years in assorted prisons. In 1957 he found a job as a security guard at a uranium mine in Utah. He had an argument with a miner, Charles Merrifield, whom he shot when they disagreed on how to grease a scoop shovel. His plea at his trial was guilty by insanity because he claimed to have syphilis. In fact, the doctors could find no trace of the disease. His execution by firing squad was the last to be carried out in the United States before capital punishment was halted by the US Supreme Court until the death penalty was reinstated in 1976.

When asked for a final statement, Rodgers continued to insist that he was innocent and said, 'I done told you my last request – a bulletproof vest.'

Ethel Rosenberg, 1915–1953
'We are the first victims of American fascism.'

On 29 March 1951 Ethel and her younger husband, Julius, both born in New York, were convicted of treason, having passed secrets of the atomic bomb to the Soviet Union. They were the only two American civilians to be executed for espionage-related activity during the Cold War.

Her final statement was, 'We are the first victims of American fascism.' She was a victim in an unexpected way. Her husband died after the first electric shock, while she survived the standard course of three. Attendants found her heart was still beating, so they administered a further two shocks, which did finally kill her.

John Eldon Smith, 1930–1983
'Well, the Lord is going to get another one.'

Smith used the alias Anthony Machetti. He and his wife decided to kill Joseph and Juanita Atkins to collect insurance money. They had separate trials and were both convicted of the murders. John Smith was executed in the electric chair at the age of fifty-three. He became the first person to be executed in Georgia since 1976, when the death penalty was reinstated. His last words were, 'Well, the Lord is going to get another one.'

John Spenkelink, 1949–1979
'Capital punishment – them without the capital get the punishment.'

A small-time criminal from Le Mars, Iowa, he shot and killed another crook called Joseph Szymankiewicz in 1973 in Tallahassee, Florida. He claimed that he acted in self-defence and turned down a plea bargain to second-degree murder which would have resulted in a life sentence. In 1976 he was convicted of first-degree murder and sentenced to death. His execution was controversial because he was the first prisoner in Florida to be executed after capital punishment was reinstated in 1976. His final words were, 'Capital punishment – them without the capital get the punishment.'

Pancho Villa, 1878–1923
'Don't let it end like this. Tell them I said something.'

Mexican revolutionary. He and his men sought to redistribute land to peasants and soldiers. He robbed trains and printed money to pay for his cause.

Villa conducted a famous raid on Columbus, New Mexico, in 1916, as a result of which US Army General John J. Pershing tried unsuccessfully to capture him in a nine-month pursuit that ended when the United States entered into the First World War. Villa retired in 1920 and was given a large estate, which he turned into a 'military colony' for his former soldiers. In 1923, he decided to reinvolve himself in Mexican politics and as a result was assassinated.

Villa was killed while visiting Parral. He had gone to collect a consignment of gold from the local bank with which to pay his ranch staff. On the way home he passed by a school. A man ran toward Villa's car and shouted, 'Viva Villa,' which was the signal for a group of seven riflemen firing over forty shots into the car. No less than nine Dumdum bullets hit Villa in the head and upper chest, killing him instantly. He was found in the driver seat of the car, with one hand reaching for his gun.

Many sources claim that his final words were, 'Don't let it end like this. Tell them I said something.' There is no evidence that this is true. Indeed, he would not have had the time or opportunity to say anything.

Dictators

Francisco Franco, 1892–1975
'¿Dónde van?'

Spanish soldier who prospered in the Spanish Civil War and was the dictator of Spain from 1939 until his death in 1975. He was in a coma from 30 October 1975 until he died on 20 November.

Nevertheless, there is an engaging story about his supposed final words. He was lying on his deathbed and thousands of supporters had gathered at the presidential palace, cheering his name. When he heard the noise he asked his doctor what it was all about and was told, 'Es tu pueblo, generalísimo.' ('It is your people, generalissimo.')

'¿Qué quieren?' ('What do they want?') Franco asked.

'Que quieren decir adios.' ('They want to say goodbye.')

Franco looked confused and asked, '¿Dónde van?' ('Where are they going?')

Muammar al-Gaddafi, 1942–2011
'Don't shoot me, don't shoot me.'

Libyan politician and revolutionary who seized power in 1969. The Arab Spring of 2011 led to a civil war in Libya, during which Gaddafi's forces steadily lost the support of the majority of the country. On 20 October he tried to break out of his stronghold at Sirte, but NATO aircraft bombed his convoy, forcing him and his personal guards to take refuge on a building site. They were found in drainage pipes and savagely beaten, stabbed and shot. Some say that his final words were, 'What did I do to you? Do you know right from wrong?' or 'Don't shoot me, don't shoot me.'

Adolf Hitler, 1889–1945
'Es lohnt sich nicht so freundlich zu sein.'

Hitler needs no introduction, even if that is for bad reasons. His rise to power could never have been predicted in 1923 when he led a coup in Munich and landed up in prison. His time as German chancellor led to a very bleak few years for Germany and the world.

As the Russians were fighting their way closer to the heart of Berlin, Hitler drew up his last will. It was a short document signed on 29 April at 4 a.m.

It acknowledged his marriage – but did not name Eva Braun – and stated that they chose death over disgrace or capitulation; their bodies were to be cremated.

His art collection was left to 'a gallery in my home town of Linz on Donau'. Objects of 'sentimental value or necessary for the maintenance of a modest simple life' went to his relatives and his 'faithful co-workers' such as secretary Mrs Winter. Whatever else of value he possessed went to the National Socialist German Workers Party.

Martin Bormann was nominated as the will's executor. The will was witnessed by Dr Joseph Goebbels, Martin Bormann and Colonel Nicholaus von Below.

Some sources claim that his final words were, 'Es lohnt sich nicht so freundlich zu sein,' ('It doesn't pay to be so kind') but there is absolutely no evidence that this is true.

Saddam Hussein, 1937–2006
'There is no God but Allah and Muhammad is God's messenger.'

Fifth President of Iraq, who served from 16 July 1979 until 9 April 2003. He was born in Al-Awha, Saladin Province in Iraq and became a leading member of the revolutionary Arab Socialist Ba'ath Party. He played a key role in the 1968 coup (later referred to as the 17 July Revolution) that brought the party to power in Iraq.

He formally rose to power in 1979, although he had been the de facto head of Iraq for several years. He suppressed Shi'a and Kurdish movements seeking to overthrow the government or gain independence, and maintained power during the Iran–Iraq War and the Gulf War.

In 2003, a coalition led by the US and UK invaded Iraq to depose Saddam, in which US President George W. Bush and British Prime Minister Tony Blair accused him of possessing weapons of mass destruction and having ties to al-Qaeda. History has shown that those claims were false.

Following his capture on 13 December 2003, the trial of Saddam took place under the Iraqi interim government. On 5 November 2006, he was convicted of charges related to the 1982 killing of 148 Iraqi Shi'ites and was sentenced to hang. His execution was carried out on 30 December 2006.

His final words to his executioners at Camp Justice in the Baghdad suburb of Khadimiya on 30 December 2006 were, 'There is no God but Allah and Muhammad is God's messenger.'

Benito Mussolini, 1883–1945
'Sparami nel petto!'

An Italian politician born in Predappio, who led the National Fascist Party and ruled the country from 1922 until he was overthrown in 1943. After destroying all political opposition through his secret police and the outlawing of labour strikes, Mussolini consolidated his power and created a one-party dictatorship. Dismissed by the king in July 1943, he was rescued in September by a special German parachute group. He understood that his life would be in danger, so decided to escape with his mistress, Petacci, to Spain via Switzerland. They were stopped by communist partisans near the village of Dongo (Lake Como).

Mussolini and Petacci were both summarily executed. The shootings took place in the small village of Giulino di Mezzegra. In their final moments, Petacci hugged Mussolini and refused to move away from him when they were taken to an empty space. Shots were fired and Petacci fell down. Just then Mussolini opened his jacket and screamed, 'Sparami nel petto!' ('Shoot me in the chest!') His executioner complied and shot him in the chest.

Pol Pot, 1925–1998
'No. I want you to know. Everything I did, I did for my country.'

Born Saloth Sar, he became the Khmer Rouge dictator of Cambodia and systematically set about killing intellectuals, the middle class and anyone who opposed him. One unreliable source claims that his final words were spoken to a reporter, who asked if he regretted his actions. The reply was, 'No. I want you to know. Everything I did, I did for my country.'

Joseph Stalin, 1879–1953
Not known

Born into a desperately poor Georgian family, Joseph Stalin began his working life as a career criminal. Particularly notable was his participation in the 1907 Tiflis bank robbery, which resulted in forty deaths and the theft of 341,000 roubles (which equates to roughly £2.5 million in today's terms). He was exiled to Siberia on seven occasions and during his final exile he was conscripted by the Russian Army to fight in the First World War, but he was declared unfit for service because of his deformed left arm.

The revolution was good for Stalin, who swiftly progressed through the Bolshevik chain of command and by the mid-1920s was effectively the leader of the country, a position he consolidated and maintained until his death in 1953. During his time in power, millions of his fellow citizens were executed, deported, imprisoned or allowed to starve.

There are many versions of Stalin's death. What is clear is that he had a severe stroke, which some suggest was deliberately caused by Beria, Malenkov, Bulganin and Khrushchev, all of whom had good reason to act because they believed (probably accurately) that they were about to be purged. They claimed that they had all dined with Stalin on the night of 28 February. Dinner finished at five or six in the morning. Nothing was heard of Stalin the next day, which was a day of rest, and he was found lying beside a sofa on the floor of his room early on the morning of 2 March. He finally died during the late evening of 5 March, but not before a final terrifying moment when he seemed to recover consciousness, raised his right hand at his colleagues in a threatening gesture, then lay back and died. Nobody recorded his final words as he went to bed in the early hours of 1 March.

Mao Tse-Tung, 1893–1976
'I feel ill. Call the doctors.'

Chairman Mao was a political revolutionary and theorist who was the founder of the People's Republic of China and leader from 1949 until his death. Some 70 million Chinese died under his leadership. At the end of July 1976, after a large earthquake in Peking, he was moved to a nondescript building in Zhongnanhai which was highly secure and earthquake-proof. He was giving the orders right up until the end, although he was bedbound. Meng, one of his former girlfriends turned nurse, reported that his final words were, 'I feel ill. Call the doctors.' He then slipped into unconsciousness and died at ten minutes past midnight on the morning of 9 September 1976.

Heroes

Thomas Hopper Alderson GC, 1903–1965
Never recorded

Alderson was an Air Raid Precautions (ARP) warden in Bridlington during the Second World War and was the first-ever recipient of the George Cross. On three separate occasions in 1940 he tunnelled through the rubble of destroyed houses to rescue people trapped in the buildings. Seventeen people were saved by his selfless action, undertaken in the most hazardous conditions. He was also awarded a medal from the RSPCA (Royal Society for the Prevention of Cruelty to Animals) later in the war for rescuing two horses from a burning stable. He died of lung cancer in a hospital in Driffield, Yorkshire, unable to speak, so his last words were never recorded.

Lieutenant-Commander Robert Selby Armitage, GC, GM, RNVR, 1905–1982.
'I can't face it anymore.'

Hero or villain? He is one of only eight people who won both the George Cross and the George Medal, for defusing unexploded bombs and mines. On 26 May 1982, at his home in Nettlebed, Oxfordshire, he shot his wife, wounding her in the head but not fatally, and then killed himself. He had been deeply depressed for a long time and said that he couldn't face it anymore.

Jacob Astor, 1864–1912
'See you in the morning.'

An American businessman born at Rhinebeck, New York. The family was already wealthy, but young Jacob had the gift of making money. He invented machinery, wrote novels and made a serious fortune in property deals. At the age of thirty-eight he personally financed the 'Astor Battery' of voluntary artillerymen who fought in the Philippines.

While the couple were touring, Madeleine Astor became pregnant. They wanted the child to be born in the USA, so they joined the *Titanic* at Cherbourg. Everyone knows what happened to the ship. Astor helped his young bride on to one of the lifeboats, and asked a ship's officer if he could keep his wife company because of her condition. He was told that men would be allowed onto the lifeboats only when all the women and children had been cared for. He said, 'See you in the morning,' to his bride and was last seen standing alone and smoking a cigarette.

Todd Beamer, 1968–2001
'Are you guys ready? Let's roll.'

A passenger on United Flight 93, on 11 September 2001. With the plane hijacked by terrorists, Beamer tried to place a credit card call through a phone located on the back of a plane seat. Beamer reported that one passenger was killed and, later, that a flight attendant had told him the pilot and co-pilot had been forced from the cockpit and may have been wounded. According to accounts of cell phone conversations, Beamer, along with Mark Bingham, Tom Burnett and Jeremy Glick, formed a plan to take the plane back from the hijackers, and led other passengers in this effort.

The plane crashed near Shanksville, Pennsylvania. His final words were, 'Are you guys ready? Let's roll.'

Donald Campbell, 1921–1967
'I've got the bows up – I'm going.'

Campbell, born at Kington-upon-Thames, was the son of Sir Malcolm Campbell, who broke thirteen world speed records. A confident and successful man, he seemed determined to exceed his father's record, and broke eight world speed records on water and on land in the 1950s and 1960s. He is the only person to set both world land and water speed records in the same year (1964).

Campbell was attempting to set a new world water speed record exceeding 300 mph. His first run was 297 mph. The crash occurred on the return run. Had he completed it, it would have been fast enough to set a record exceeding 300 mph. The final radio transmission from *Bluebird K7* as she lifted from the surface of Coniston Water, flipped bow over stern and smashed to pieces on the lake surface in January 1967 was, 'I've got the bows up – I'm going.'

Edith Cavell, 1865–1915
'I have no fear or shrinking; I have seen death so often it is not strange, or fearful to me.'

Born in Norfolk, Cavell went into nursing and developed her skills in Belgium. By chance she was visiting her mother in Norfolk when the First World War broke out, but she returned to Brussels to carry on with her job.

In November 1914 the Germans occupied the city and she started to give shelter to French and British soldiers before passing them along an escape route to get back home. The Germans were already suspicious when a collaborator gave her away. She was arrested for and tried for treason. A British chaplain, the Reverend Gahan, reported Cavell's words: 'I have no fear or shrinking; I have seen death so often it is not strange, or fearful to me.' This may have been some time before the execution itself. Another source reports her words were, 'Standing, as I do, in the view of God and eternity I realize that patriotism is not enough. I must have no hatred or bitterness towards anyone.'

Noel Chavasse, VC and Bar, MC, 1884–1917
'Please tell Gladys, my fiancée, that duty called me and called me to obey.'

Captain Noel Chavasse was a extraordinary man. One of twins, he graduated with a first-class degree in philosophy from Trinity College, Oxford. While at university, he earned his blue in both athletics and lacrosse. He and his twin, Christopher, represented Great Britain in the 400 metres at the 1908 Olympic Games. He became the medical officer of the 10th (Liverpool Scottish) Battalion, the King's (Liverpool) Regiment, during the first three years of the First World War and was the only man to win the Victoria Cross twice during the Great War.

Only two other men have achieved this honour. Captain Arthur Martin-Leake won his first VC during the Boer War in 1901 and his second in 1915 during the First World War; both men were in the Royal Army Medical Corps. The second was Captain Charles Upham, a New Zealander serving with 20th Bn, 2nd NZEF (the Canterbury Regiment) who won his first VC as a second lieutenant in Crete between 22 and 30 May 1941 and his Bar on 14/15 July 1942 in the Western Desert as a captain. By chance, Chavasse and Upham were distantly related by marriage.

The popular tradition is that his last words were, 'Please tell Gladys, my fiancée, that duty called me and called me to obey,' and it is true that his fiancé was Gladys Chavasse, who was his cousin.

Davy Crockett, 1786–1836
'I warn you boys, I'm a screamer.'

American folk hero from Tennessee, commonly known as the 'King of the Wild Frontier.' Historians have been unable to agree whether he was killed in combat or executed by General Santa Ana at the Battle of the Alamo in Texas. Some sources claim that he was killed on the orders of Santa Ana, who would accept no prisoners. In that tale, Crockett supposedly said, 'I warn you boys, I'm a screamer.' But it is far more likely that he died in action and one report says that his body was found with sixteen Mexican corpses around him. His mother, when she heard of his death, famously said, 'I bet he had no wounds in his back.'

Raymond Donoghue, GC, 1920–1960
'Get back.'

Donoghue was an Australian tram conductor posthumously awarded the George Cross for the gallantry he displayed in Hobart, Tasmania. On 29 April 1960, he was the conductor of a tram which collided with a lorry, incapacitating the tram's driver. The tram began to roll down the main road, quickly gathering speed. Donoghue worked his way to the cab, shifted the driver and struggled to apply the brakes but without success. He stayed in the driver's cab and his final words were to order the passengers to the back of the vehicle while ringing the bell to warn traffic. Eventually the tram ran straight into another tram, killing Donoghue. Forty-seven passengers were injured.

Edith Evans, 1875–1912
'You go first. You have children waiting for you.'

On the *Titanic* she was one of a group of women and children waiting for instructions to join a lifeboat. Miss Evans determined that Mrs John Murray Brown should have priority and said, 'You go first. You have children waiting for you.'

Sergeant Stewart Guthrie, GC, 1948–1990
'Stop, David, or I shoot.'

Guthrie was a New Zealand police sergeant from Dunedin. On 13 November 1990 he was the duty officer at Port Chalmers police station when there was a report of a man firing a weapon in Aramoana, a small town some eight kilometres away. It was said that he had killed several people (in fact he killed thirteen before he was shot dead himself).

Sergeant Guthrie immediately went to the town. He took with him a police Smith & Wesson revolver. By chance he knew the gunman, David Gray, and found him at his house. Guthrie posted a police colleague at the front of the house, while he himself went to the rear. Gray tried to escape through the front of the house but retreated back inside when challenged. He then exited through the rear of his house. Guthrie challenged him with what proved to be his final words, 'Stop, David, or I shoot', and fired a warning shot into the air. The gunman responded by shooting Guthrie dead.

Barbara Jane Harrison, GC, 1945–1968
'There are more people to help.'

Harrison is the only female to be awarded the George Cross for gallantry in peacetime. On 8 April 1968, BOAC Flight 712 to Sydney left Heathrow Airport. Within minutes, the aircraft's number two engine caught fire and fell from the port wing. The pilot managed to land almost immediately but fire grew more intense and spread to the fuselage. Harrison, who was a flight attendant, together with another steward, inflated the escape chute at the rear of the plane but it failed to deploy properly and the steward had to climb down to free it. Once on the ground, he was unable to return.

Harrison continued to help passengers to escape as the fire spread. Eventually escape from the rear of the aircraft became impossible and she directed the remaining passengers to another exit. She refused to leave the plane to save herself, saying, 'There are more people to help.' Her body was found near that of a disabled pensioner, seated in one of the last rows.

Sergeant Murray Hudson, GC, 1938–1974
'Throw it, just throw it.'

Born in Opotiki in the Bay of Plenty, Hudson enlisted in the New Zealand Army in 1961 and served as a soldier in the New Zealand Special Air Service in Malaya, Borneo and Vietnam. When he was working as a drill instructor at Waiouru, he supervised a training exercise during which a young soldier accidentally armed a grenade he was about to throw. Hudson saw that the soldier couldn't react and immediately shouted, 'Throw it, just throw it.' The soldier failed to obey so Hudson grasped his hand and tried to release the grenade, which exploded, killing them both.

Major Anders Larssen, VC, MC and two Bars, 1920–1945
'Leave me.'

One of three Danes to be awarded the Victoria Cross. The *London Gazette* published the citation for the Victoria Cross on 4 September 1945 and this is a precis of what it said.

On the night of 8 April 1945, Anders was ordered to take out a patrol on the north shore of Lake Comacchio. His tasks were to cause as many casualties and as much confusion as possible, to give the impression of a major landing, and to capture prisoners. His group was challenged and pretended to be fishermen returning home, but the ruse didn't work and they came under heavy machine-gun fire. Anders led the attack with grenades and took out the first nest. He ignored the withering fire from three other machine-gun positions and dashed forward to take out a second nest. In both cases his men followed him in to take the positions for themselves. Larssen then went forward to take the third nest but was hit by machine-gun fire to his left. He fell, mortally wounded, but still managed to throw another grenade which allowed his men to quell the resistance in the third nest.

The remains of his much-reduced team prepared to evacuate him but he absolutely refused to go, claiming it would impede the withdrawal and endanger the lives of his men. They had to leave the area anyway because they had run out of ammunition. Larssen died where he lay.

Daniel Marvin, 1894–1912
'It's all right, little girl. You go. I will stay.'

Daniel and Mary Marvin boarded the *Titanic* at Southampton as first-class passengers. They were returning to New York City from their honeymoon in Europe. When the evacuation began, Daniel led his bride to one of the lifeboats, saying, 'It's all right, little girl. You go. I will stay.'

Florence Nightingale, OM, RRC, 1820–1910
'Bless the Lord, oh my soul.'

Born in Florence and, like her elder sister, named after the city in which she was born. She fell out with her mother and sister, who expected a woman of her social standing to become a wife and mother. Instead she elected to become a nurse. She is often called the founder of modern nursing. During the Crimean War, she was dubbed 'the Lady with the Lamp' after her habit of making rounds at night.

She died peacefully in her sleep in London. Her nurses and doctor were prepared for the event, and assorted statements were noted. When her doctor appeared, she said, 'Bless the Lord, oh my soul.' One nurse reported that shortly before she died, she smiled, waving her hand overhead as if to say, 'It's all right. I'm dying.'

It is helpful to draw upon two of the recorded statements made earlier in her life: 'I attribute my success to this – I never gave or took any excuse.' And, aptly for the modern age, taken from her *Notes on Nursing*: 'The very first requirement in a hospital is that it should do the sick no harm.'

Flight Lieutenant John Quinton, GC, DFC, 1921–1951
'Jump.'

Born at Brockley near Lewisham, Quinton served in the RAF during the war then left to go into industry in 1946. He married and had a son but decided that civilian life was not for him and rejoined the Air Force as a flight lieutenant. Just two months after rejoining, he was the navigator in a Wellington aircraft which was involved in a mid-air collision on 13 August 1951. With him in a rear compartment was a sixteen-year-old air training cadet, Derek Coates. When the impact caused the Wellington to break up, Quinton picked up the only parachute available, clipped it on to the cadet's harness, showed him how to pull the ripcord and ordered, 'Jump.' The cadet landed safely. All eight other occupants of the two planes died.

Ayrton Senna, 1960–1994
'The car seems okay … '

A Brazilian racing driver from Sao Paolo who won three Formula One world championships. The 1994 San Marino Grand Prix was beset with many problems, including the earlier death during practice of the Austrian, Ratzenberger. Senna's protégé, Rubens Barichello, had a bad crash during the qualifying session, and Senna's own car seemed to have steering problems. Moreover, the race itself had to be restarted after a large crash on the start line.

He was leading the race ahead of Michael Schumacher and in conversation with his pit team, he radioed, 'The car seems okay ... ' A few seconds later his steering column broke and he died when his car hit a concrete wall at 145 mph. It is believed that the right suspension frame was sent stabbing back into the cockpit, striking Senna on the right side of his helmet, forcing his head back against the headrest and causing fatal skull fractures and brain injury.

Sir Ernest Shackleton, 1874–1922
'You are always wanting me to give up things – what is it I ought to give up?'

Shackleton was an inspirational leader of men, although some thought he was a charlatan. Born in Ireland, he led three British expeditions to Antarctica. In January 1909 he and three companions established a record Farthest South latitude at 88° 23' S, which was just 97 geographical miles (112 statute miles, 180 km) from the South Pole. King Edward VII knighted him for the success.

On his next expedition, from 1914–1917, his ship, *Endurance*, became trapped in pack ice and was slowly crushed. This catastrophe led to a prolonged stay on an ice floe which they hoped would find landfall at Paulet Island, 250 miles away. When the floe broke up, the party took to their boats and eventually landed at Elephant Island, 346 miles from where *Endurance* sank.

Knowing that he had to take positive action, Shackleton determined to travel some 800 miles in an open boat to South Georgia. He took five volunteers and, after fifteen days in terrible weather, found their target, eventually landing on the south shore. Shackleton with two of his team then travelled 32 miles across harsh mountainous terrain in thirty-six hours to reach the whaling station at Stromness on 20 May 1916. This allowed him to arrange the rescue of his crew on Elephant Island, who, it must be said, never doubted his success. It was an astonishing and courageous feat.

His last expedition, the Shackleton–Rowett Expedition, left England on 24 September 1921. By January they were back in South Georgia, where Shackleton complained of back pain and other ailments. He called for the expedition's physician, Alexander Macklin. He told his 'boss' that he had been doing too much and ought to lead a more regular life. To this,

Shackleton responded, 'You are always wanting me to give up things – what is it I ought to give up?' He never heard Macklin's answer, which was, 'Chiefly alcohol, Boss, I don't think it agrees with you.' At 2.50 a.m. on 5 January 1922, Shackleton died of a fatal heart attack.

Violette Szabo, GC, 1921–1945
Not recorded

No list of heroes would be complete without the name of Violette Szabo, born Violette Bushell in Paris on 26 June 1921. After her husband died at the Battle of El Alamein, she volunteered for and was recruited into SOE, where she proved to be an enormously popular and brave colleague. Odette Churchill, GC, said of her, 'She was the bravest of us all.'

She was captured at Salon-la-Tour on 10 June 1944, just three days after starting her second SOE mission. Her captors interrogated and tortured her before she was transported to Ravensbruck concentration camp, where she was executed by firing squad on 5 February 1945 aged just twenty-three. The fact is that nobody can say what her final words were. However, Leo Marks composed a now famous poem for Szabo to use as part of her code structure. It was used in the film about Szabo, *Carve Her Name with Pride*, and deliberately attributed to her husband, Etienne. Marks did not want the real author to be identified:

> The life that I have
> Is all that I have
> And the life that I have
> Is yours.
> The love that I have
> Of the life that I have
> Is yours and yours and yours.
> A sleep I shall have
> A rest I shall have
> Yet death will be but a pause.
> For the peace of my years
> In the long green grass
> Will be yours and yours and yours.

The Violette Szabo Museum is at 'Cartref', Wormelow, Herefordshire.

Elisabeth von Thadden, 1890–1944
'Setzen Sie ein Ende, o Gott, für alle unsere Leiden.'

Pomeranian teacher who was active in the anti-Hitler movement. After being forced to close her flourishing school in Heidelberg in 1941, she turned to work with the Red Cross and joined the Resistance. On 10 September 1943 she hosted a meeting at her house to discuss the Nazi regime. One young man who attended the meeting, having been invited by an old friend, reported her and her guests to the Gestapo. She was sentenced to death by the Volksgericht and was executed on 8 September 1944. Her last words were, 'Setzen Sie ein Ende, o Gott, für alle unsere Leiden.' ('Put an end, O Lord, to all our sufferings.')

Scientists

Archimedes, 287–212 BC
'Wait till I have finished my problem.'

The man from Syracuse whose scientific mind still informs modern day mathematics.

During the Siege of Syracuse, he was ordered by a soldier to follow him for a meeting with General Marcellus. Archimedes said, 'Wait till I have finished my problem.' The soldier was enraged and killed him with his sword.

Another suggestion is that he said, 'Do not disturb my circles.' The fact is that nobody can say with any certainty and the man who wrote about the siege, Plutarch, was born more than 250 years after Archimedes' death.

Alexander Graham Bell, 1847–1922
'No.'

The eminent scientist and inventor from Edinburgh who invented the first practical telephone. Acoustics were his early interest, in part because his mother was deaf. He had diabetes, which increasingly degraded his health. His wife, Mabel, tended to him throughout and it is said that seconds before he died, she whispered, 'Don't leave me.' Bell's last act was to trace the sign for 'no'.

Luther Burbank, 1849–1926
'I don't feel good.'

Burbank was born in Lancaster, Massachusetts; he was the thirteenth child of his farming parents. His father died when young Luther was twenty-one, leaving him a legacy, with which he bought a plot of land and developed a disease-resistant potato, still known as the Burbank potato; it is extensively used in food processing. This was the first success in a horticultural career which produced over 800 strains and varieties of plants.

He had a heart attack in late March of 1926 and died on 11 April. His last recorded words were, 'I don't feel good.'

Nicholas Copernicus, 1473–1543
'Now, O Lord, set Thy servant free.'

Polish Renaissance mathematician and astronomer, who evolved the theory that the sun was the centre of the universe, not the Earth. As he approached the end of his life, he was seized by apoplexy and paralysis. Legend has it that he was presented with an advance copy of his *De revolutionibus orbium coelestium* (*On the Revolutions of the Celestial Spheres*) on the very day that he died, allowing him to bid farewell to his life's work. He is reputed to have awoken from a stroke-induced coma, looked at his book, and then died peacefully. Some sources claim that he uttered the words, 'Now, O Lord, set Thy servant free.'

Baron Georges Cuvier, 1769–1832
'Infirmière, c'est moi qui ai découvert que les sangsues ont le sang rouge.'

French naturalist and zoologist born in Montbéliard, some 13 kilometres from the Swiss border of eastern France. Cuvier dedicated himself to natural sciences research and helped to establish the fields of comparative anatomy and palaeontology. He died in Paris during a cholera epidemic. His last words were reported as, 'Infirmière, c'est moi qui ai découvert que les sangsues ont le sang rouge.' ('Nurse, it was I who discovered that leeches have red blood.')

Charles Darwin, FRS, 1809–1882
'It's almost worthwhile to be sick to be nursed by you.'

The English naturalist from Shrewsbury who, to the intense resistance of the scientific community, proposed that all life descended over time from common ancestors. He defined the process we know as natural selection. He died at his home, Down House, of a heart attack on 19 April 1882. His last words were to his family, telling his wife, Emma, 'I am not the least afraid of death – remember what a good wife you have been to me – tell all my children to remember how good they have been to me.' Then he said to his children, Henrietta and Francis, 'It's almost worthwhile to be sick to be nursed by you.'

Brewer's *Dictionary of Phrase and Fable* disagrees with the record, claiming that his final words were, 'I am not in the least afraid to die.'

George Eastman, 1854–1932
'To my friends: my work is done. Why wait?'

The American inventor was born in Waterville, New York. He established Eastman Kodak and invented roll film. He was a significant philanthropist, establishing the Eastman School of Music and funding clinics in London and other European cities to serve people with low incomes. In his latter years he experienced chronic pain and limited movement because of a spinal illness. On 14 March 1932 he shot himself, leaving a suicide note which read, 'To my friends: My work is done. Why wait?'

Thomas Alva Edison, 1847–1931
'It's beautiful over there.'

Edison was born in Milan, Ohio, and was the seventh child of Samuel Edison, who fled from Canada after taking part in the unsuccessful Mackenzie Rebellion in 1837. He seemed to be a bit of a dreamer at school, which led to an early end to his formal education. But the wandering mind was really busy inventing things. Happily he was also a good businessman so he was able to make a commercial success of his many ideas. Among the 1,093 items which have US patents in his name are the phonograph, the motion picture camera and the electric light bulb. Edison is the fourth most prolific inventor in history.

He died of complications of diabetes on 18 October 1931 in his home, 'Glenmont' in New Jersey. Apparently, his last words were, 'It is very beautiful over there.'

Albert Einstein, 1879–1955
'It's time to go. I will do it elegantly.'

Born at Ulm in Germany, Einstein was a physicist who established the general theory of relativity. In 1921 he received the Nobel Prize for Physics.

On 17 April 1955, an abdominal aortic aneurysm ruptured. He had undergone surgery on the problem in 1948. In an orderly fashion, he was taken to hospital, taking with him the draft of a speech he was preparing. He did not live long enough to complete it. He refused surgery, saying, 'I want to go when I want. It is tasteless to prolong life artificially. I have done my share, it is time to go. I will do it elegantly.'

Some sources quote his final words as 'Citater fra ... ', which were actually in the speech that he was drafting.

Richard Feynman, 1918–1988
'I'd hate to die twice. It's so boring.'

An American theoretical physicist from Manhattan whose career was in quantum mechanics. He was part of the team that developed the atomic bomb. Unfortunately he contracted two rare forms of cancer and died shortly after an unsuccessful operation to address one of them. He is reported to have said, 'I'd hate to die twice. It's so boring.'

Joseph Henry Green, 1791–1863
'It's stopped.'

The son of a merchant in the City of London, Green lived a very comfortable life thanks to the legacy of his father. He became a surgeon and was appointed as the literary executor of Samuel Taylor Coleridge. Some six weeks before he died, he had a severe stroke and it is unclear whether or when he said, 'It's stopped,' upon checking his own pulse.

Werner Heisenburg, 1901–1976
'Ich werde ihn fragen, warum gibt es Turbulenzen.'

Born in Wurzburg, a medieval walled town on the Romantische Strasse, Heisenburg was the son of a teacher of classical languages. He studied mathematics and physics and became a theoretical physicist who was awarded the Nobel Prize for Physics in 1932 'for the creation of quantum mechanics'. He died of cancer of the kidneys and gall bladder at his home, on 1 February 1976. We cannot say with any certainty what the circumstances were when he said, 'Ich werde ihn fragen, warum gibt es Turbulenzen.' ('I will ask Him why there is turbulence.')

Dave Johnston, 1949–1980
'Vancouver, Vancouver. This is it!'

Dave Johnston was born in Chicago to hard-working parents, one of whom, his mother, was a journalist. This seemed an attractive profession, but he gained poor marks in the subject so, in what may seem to be a leap of faith, he changed his course to geology and became a volcanologist with the United States Geological Survey (USGS).

He was killed by the 1980 eruption of Mount St Helens in Washington. He was installed in an observation post some 6 miles (10 km) from the volcano on the morning of 18 May 1980. He was the first person to report the eruption, transmitting the message, 'Vancouver! Vancouver! This is it!' At that moment the mountain's northern face collapsed, creating the blast that killed him.

Pierre Simon Laplace, 1749–1827
'Ce que nous savons, c'est peu, et ce que nous ignorons est immense.'
Born into a Norman farming family, Laplace became a mathematician and astronomer who is often said to be the French equivalent of Isaac Newton. According to Joseph Fourier, another French mathematician, his last words, uttered with immense difficulty, were, 'Ce que nous savons, c'est peu, et ce que nous ignorons est immense.' ('What we know is little, and what we are ignorant of is immense.')

Michel de Nostradame (commonly known as Nostradamus), 1503–1566
'Vous ne me trouverez pas vivant au lever du soleil.'
Michel was one of at least nine children whose parents were of Jewish origin but converted to Catholicism in 1455. Trained as a doctor, he became increasingly interested in the occult and published an almanac in 1550 with a number of predictions. It was a success, so he continued to produce it annually. Ultimately, he published 6,338 prophesies. Most are in the form of quatrains predicting disaster.

On the evening of 2 July 1566, he is alleged to have told his secretary, 'Vous ne me trouverez pas vivant au lever du soleil.' ('You will not find me alive at sunrise.') The next morning he was found dead, lying on the floor next to his bed.

Pythgoras, 570–495BC
'Don't disarrange my circles.'
Ionian Greek philosopher born in Samos. He was a mathematician who articulated a theorem that still bears his name, although modern scholars are not at all convinced that he was responsible for it. Indeed, his name was first associated with it five hundred years after his death.

The truth is that nobody has a clear idea about the man or his work and the common attribution of the final words, 'Don't disarrange my circles,' can only be a modern invention. Interestingly, Archimedes is also credited with the same final words.

Edward Teller, 1908–2003
'I should have been a concert pianist.'

Teller was born in Budapest and always had a natural facility with numbers. He became a physicist and was deeply associated with the development of the hydrogen bomb.

He emigrated to the United States in 1935 and accepted the appointment as Professor of Physics at George Washington University. After the start of the war, he was swiftly involved in the Manhattan Project. However, he became unpopular with the scientific community because he had testified against Oppenheimer, claiming he was a security risk.

He lived to the age of ninety-five and died without fanfare. Some record his final words as, 'I should have been a concert pianist.'

William Wilde, 1815–1876
'Oh, those boys, those boys.'

The youngest of three sons from Castlerea in Co. Roscommon, William Wilde became a surgeon and was the father of Oscar Wilde. He married Jane Francesca Agnes Elgee, who wrote and published poetry under the name of Speranza. Young Oscar had a brother, Willie, and a sister, Isola Francesca, who died in childhood. He also had three illegitimate children (a boy and two girls) conceived before his marriage. He died in some disgrace at the age of sixty-one after he was accused of seducing one of his patients, who happened to be the daughter of a colleague, saying, 'Oh, those boys, those boys.'

Politicians and Statesmen

Lady Nancy Astor, 1879–1964
'Am I dying, or is it my birthday?'

Born Nancy Langhorne in Virginia, she was one of eleven children. She married her first husband, Robert Shaw, when she was eighteen. It was not a success and lasted only four years. Her second husband was the adoptive Englishman Waldorf Astor, who was born on the same day as his bride, 19 May 1879. She was the first woman to sit as an MP in the House of Commons and was famous for her scathing wit. On her deathbed with her family gathered about her, she is alleged to have said, 'Am I dying, or is it my birthday?'

George C. Atcheson, 1886–1947
'Well, it can't be helped.'

Atcheson was the chief US political adviser to the Japan Occupation Forces, flying on a plane with nine others. They were only 65 miles west of Hawaii when the plane ran out of fuel. When he realised that they were going to crash into the Pacific, his final words were, 'Well, it can't be helped.' His words were reported by one of the three survivors.

Augustus, the first Roman Emperor, 63 BC–AD 14
'Numquid ego functum bene? Applaudunt bonus tunc sicut.'

Born Gaius Octavius, his stroke of luck was to be named by his great uncle, Julius Caesar, as his adoptive son and heir. He proved to be an astute politician and soldier and worked his way inexorably to become the first Roman Emperor.

There is an allegation that Augustus died by eating poisoned figs. Tiberius, who was present at Augustus' deathbed, was named his heir and reported the Emperor's last words as, 'Numquid ego functum bene? Applaudunt bonus

tunc sicut.' ('Have I played the part well? Then applaud as I exit.') In public, though, his last words were published as, 'Behold, I found Rome of clay, and leave her to you of marble.'

Max Aitken, First Baron Beaverbrook, 1879–1964
'Maybe I would not wake up.'

A serial entrepreneur, Aitken was born in Canada and made his first fortune by creating then selling his interest in Canada Cement. He moved to England and became the Unionist Member of Parliament for Ashton-under-Lyne. His second fortune was accrued through his purchase of Charles Rolls shares in Rolls-Royce. His plans to take control of the business were resisted by the managing director, so he sold his interest and transferred his focus to newspapers. He owned the *Daily Express*, *Sunday Express* and *London Evening Standard*.

In 1918 he became Britain's first Minister of Information and in the Second World War he was Minister of Aircraft Production and Minister of Supply.

He was not universally popular, but he was a determined philanthropist and established the Beaverbrook Foundation, which continues today.

Riddled with cancer, he died in Surrey. His last words were, 'Maybe I would not wake up,' in response to the advice that he should take a rest.

Otto von Bismarck, 1815–1898
'Ich wünschte, ich konnte Johanna wieder sehen.'

Bismarck was the child of a wealthy estate owner with lands in Schonhausen, west of Berlin. He was an urbane and charming young man who gave up his burgeoning legal career to chase a couple of pretty girls. He entered politics and in due course became the highly effective Prime Minister of Prussia (1862–73, 1873–90). He went on to establish the reality of the German Empire and became its first chancellor (1871–90). He fell from power when two kaisers died in quick succession, leaving Bismarck the challenge of dealing with Wilhelm II, who wanted to be his own man.

He enjoyed a very happy marriage with Johanna von Puttkamer, who helped him to consolidate his own personal faith. He died after spending his final years writing his memoirs. His final words were, 'Ich wünschte, ich konnte Johanna wieder sehen.' ('I wish I could see Johanna again.') His most enduring final words are enshrined on his tomb. They were aimed at Kaiser Wilhelm II: 'Hier liegt der wahre Diener des Kaisers Wilhelm I.' ('Here lies the true servant of the Emperor Wilhelm I.')

Edmund Burke, 1729–1797
'God bless you.'

Richard Burke was a prosperous Dublin solicitor who had a son, Edmund, and daughter Juliana. Curiously, the brother was brought up an Anglican and the daughter a Roman Catholic.

He entered the British Parliament as an MP in 1765. He was an uncomfortable colleague, favouring the grievances of the American colonies and taking his time to criticise the French Revolution. Winston Churchill wrote of him, 'On the one hand Burke is revealed as a foremost apostle of Liberty, on the other as the redoubtable champion of Authority.'

He anticipated his death at least a year in advance, stating firmly that his stomach was 'ruined'. His final words were, 'God bless you.'

Gaius Caligula, AD 12–41
'Me vivere.'

Born in Antium, the son of Germanicus, he succeeded his great-uncle and adoptive grandfather, Tiberius, in AD 37. He is remembered as a cruel tyrant, although modern scholarship questions the legend. Nevertheless, he was the first Roman Emperor to be assassinated. According to Tacitus, the conspirators, led by Cassius Chaerea, who was the first to stab Caligula, included a wide spectrum of the governing class. Legend suggests that his final words were, 'Me vivere.' ('I am still alive.')

Viscount Castlereagh, 1769–1822
'Bankhead, let me fall into your arms, it is all over.'

Robert Stewart, the 2nd Marquess of Londonderry, was more widely known by his courtesy title, Viscount Castlereagh. He was British Foreign Secretary at the time of Napoleon and was a crucial mover in bringing him down. He was the principal British diplomat at the Congress of Vienna.

In his final year, he seemed to have a breakdown, possibly as a result of gout combined with the stress of public criticism. At the time, he said, 'My mind, is, as it were, gone.' During his final audience with King George IV he revealed that he thought he was being blackmailed for homosexuality.

After his return home, his anxious wife removed all the items she could find that he might use to injure himself. Despite that, on 12 August he managed to find a pen knife and cut his own throat. By chance his doctor was present and reported that his patient said, 'Bankhead, let me fall into your arms, it is all over.'

Marcus Porcius Cato the Younger, 95–46 BC
'Ego autem sum Dominus ad me.'

A gifted and respected orator, he was noted for his stubbornness and tenacity, especially in his lengthy conflict with Julius Caesar. He had clearly defined moral intergrity, was immune to bribes and resisted corruption.

He committed suicide in April 46 BC. It was reported that he attempted to kill himself with his own sword, but failed to do the job properly. He was found by others in his house, including his physician, who moved to push his bowels back into the gaping stomach. Cato pushed him away and tore open the wound.

Some sources claim that before committing suicide, he sharpened the point of his sword and said, 'Ego autem sum Dominus ad me.' ('Now I am master of myself.')

Camillo de Cavour, 1810–1861
'Napoleon!'

The child of landowners, born in Turin, he was a driving force in the unification of Italy. After the declaration of a united Kingdom of Italy, Cavour took office as Italy's first Prime Minister; he died after only three months in office.

His final illness, which is thought to have been malaria, was not helped by eternal insomnia. He insisted upon being bled many times, leaving him without the resources to resist his disease. When it was known that the doctors could do no more for him, the family called for the friar Giacomo to offer the last rites. He said to the friar, 'È giunto il momento di partenza.' ('The time for departure is come.') His last words were, 'La cosa sta succedendo; essere certi che ora la cosa sta succedendo,' ('The thing is happening; be certain that now the thing is happening.') with regard to the independence of Italy. As he gradually sank he was periodically heard to mutter, 'Italia, Roma, Venezia.' Then, as if he were being greeted on the other side, his last word was spoken in the form of a salutation: 'Napoleon!'

Anton Cermak, 1873–1933
'I am glad it was me instead of you.'

An American politician of Czech origin who was Mayor of Chicago from 1931 until he was assassinated in 1933. Cermak won 58 per cent of the poll in the 1931 election, beating the incumbent 'Big Bill' Thompson, who was a flamboyant and corrupt buffoon who had failed to clean up organised crime in the city.

On 15 February 1933 he was shaking hands with Franklin D. Roosevelt at Bayfront Park, Miami, Florida, when Guiseppe Zangara tried to shoot Roosevelt. A woman called Lilian Cross saw what he was about to do and hit his arm with her handbag, disrupting his aim. Cermak was hit in the lung and died on 6 March, partly because of the gunshot wound and partly because of complications induced by colitis. Four other people were wounded and a woman died as a result of the shooting. The myth is that Cermak said to Roosevelt, who was at that stage the President-elect, 'I am glad it was me instead of you.'

Hugo Chávez, 1954–2013
'Yo no quiero morir, por favor no me dejen morir.'

A career military officer who established the secretive Revolutionary

Bolivarian Movement-200 (MBR-200) in the early 1980s with a view to overthrowing the government. His 1992 coup failed and he was imprisoned. Released after two years, he founded a socialist political party, the Fifth Republic Movement, and was elected President of Venezuela in 1998. He was re-elected in 2000, and in 2006 with over 60 per cent of the vote. On 7 October 2012, Chávez was re-elected for a fourth term. He was severely ill with cancer and receiving treatment in Cuba. According to the head of the Presidential Guard, Chávez ultimately died from a massive heart attack. Gen. Jose Ornella said that near the end of his life Chávez could not speak aloud, but mouthed, 'Yo no quiero morir, por favor no me dejen morir.' ('I don't want to die. Please don't let me die.')

Sir Winston Churchill, KG, OM, CH, TD, PC, DL, FRS, Hon. RA, 1874–1965
'I'm bored with it all.'

British Conservative politician and statesman revered for his wartime leadership although deeply criticised for much of his earlier political career, particularly during the First World War. On 15 January 1965, he suffered a severe stroke that left him gravely ill. He died at his London home nine days later, at the age of ninety, seventy years to the day after his father's death. Allegedly his last words were, 'I'm bored with it all.'

Marcus Tullius Cicero, 106–46 BC
'Nihil agis de re propria, miles, sed bene velle me occidere.'

A Roman philosopher, politician, lawyer, orator and consul (in 63 BC). He came from a wealthy family of the Roman equestrian order, and was recognised as one of Rome's greatest orators. He was an outspoken critic of the Second Triumvirate, who were determined to take revenge upon him. He was caught on 7 December 43 BC leaving his villa to take a ship destined for Macedonia. When his killers arrived, Cicero's slaves denied seeing him, but he was betrayed by a former slave of his brother.

Cicero's last words are said to have been, 'Nihil agis de re propria, miles, sed bene velle me occidere.' ('There is nothing proper about what you are doing, soldier, but do try to kill me properly.') Other sources claim that his final word was 'Percute.' ('Strike.')

Georges Clemenceau, 1841–1929
'Cette fois, ce sera une longue.'

Clemenceau served as the Prime Minister of France from 1906 to 1909, and again from 1917 to 1920. He was one of the principal architects of the Treaty of Versailles at the Paris Peace Conference. On 19 February 1919, during the Paris Peace Conference, as he was leaving his house to attend a meeting at the Crillon, a man jumped out and fired several shots at his car. One bullet hit Clemenceau between the ribs, just missing his vital organs. Too dangerous to remove, the bullet remained with him for the remainder of his life.

We can only speculate about the circumstances of his supposed final words, which were, 'Cette fois, ce sera une longue.' ('This time it will be a long one.')

Emperor Constantine, AD 272–337
'Ignoscis me?'

Constantine – as the first Christian Emperor – is a significant figure in the history of Christianity. The Church of the Holy Sepulchre, built on his orders at the purported site of Jesus' tomb in Jerusalem, became the holiest place in Christendom. In the book *Secrets of the Dead*, Tom Harper asserts that Constantine's last words were said to Gaius Valerius Maximus: 'Ignoscis me?' ('Do you forgive me?')

Oliver Cromwell, 1599–1658
'My faith is all in God.'

Born in Huntingdon to a moderately prosperous family, he showed no obvious ambition in his first forty years but became a successful military and political leader. He died as the Lord Protector of the Commonwealth of England, Scotland and Ireland. The most likely cause of death was septicaemia.

Many sources say that his final words were, 'It is not my design to drink or to sleep, but my design is to make what haste I can to be gone.'

Antonia Fraser, in her excellent biography, *Cromwell, Our Chief of Men*, explores the final days of his life and adds a range of credible statements, many of them with an emphasis on religion. In his final hours, he told those about him to 'Go on cheerfully', urging them to banish sadness altogether, and treat his death as no more to them than that of a serving-man. As he was slipping into unconsciousness once more, he told them that his own faith was all in God.

Georges Danton, 1759–1794
'Montreras ma tête au peuple. Il vaut le détour.'

Danton was born in Arcis-Sur-Aube and received a good education before taking up a career as an advocate in Paris. He was president of the Cordeliers Club, which promoted the notion of government through the consent of the people. They became an authoritative voice in the early stages of the Revolution.

Inevitably he made enemies in a world that was characterised by mistrust and conflict. Evidence of corruption was presented or manufactured. He was put on trial by the Revolutionary Tribunal and sentenced to death. His last words to the crowd were, 'Mon seul regret est que je vais avant que le rat Robespierre,' ('My only regret is that I am going before that rat Robespierre') and his final words were, 'Montreras ma tête au peuple. Il vaut le détour.' ('Show my head to the people. It is worth seeing.')

Thomas Cromwell, 1485–1540
'I die in the traditional faith.'

The son of a blacksmith, Thomas Cromwell was born in Putney. He became a lawyer and was taken into the service of Cardinal Wolsey, rising to be his secretary in 1529. The fall of Wolsey was a setback, but he managed to enter Parliament as the member for Taunton and caught the king's eye. Created 1st Earl of Essex, he was ultimately chief minister to King Henry VIII from 1532 to 1540.

The king entrusted the annulment of his marriage to Catherine of Aragon and his consequent remarriage to Anne Boleyn to Cromwell, but he served a

hard master and was condemned to death without trial. He was beheaded on Tower Hill on 28 July 1540, the day of the King's marriage to Catherine Howard.

Cromwell made a speech on the scaffold, professing to die 'in the traditional faith'.

Charles James Fox, 1749–1806
'I die happy.'

Fox came from an aristocratic background. His father was the 1st Baron Holland and his maternal grandfather was the 2nd Duke of Richmond. He was the arch rival of William Pitt the Younger. A canny political animal, he seems to have had little interest in the exercise of power and was judged to be an unlikely party leader. But he was eloquent and mentally swift and fought his corner tenaciously. He was given to excess with women, drinking and gambling. Indeed, he is said to have lost £200,000 during his life, a sum which equates to some £13 million in today's terms.

He died in office as Foreign Secretary. An autopsy revealed a hardened liver, thirty-five gallstones and around seven pints of transparent fluid in his abdomen. Apparently his last words were, 'I die happy,' although Brewer's *Dictionary of Phrase and Fable* claims that he said to his wife, 'It don't signify, my dearest, dearest Liz.'

Indira Gandhi, 1917–1984
'Namaste.'

Gandhi was the only child of Jawaharlal Nehru, the first prime minister of independent India, and she herself was the third prime minister, serving for three consecutive terms from 1966 to 1977, then for a fourth term from 1980 to 1984.

The *Sikh Times* and *Time* magazine on 12 November 1984 reported on the death of Gandhi as follows:

> She was in a buoyant mood as she opened the door of her private bungalow on the morning of her assassination. She walked onto a winding gravel path toward the larger building in the complex. Following discreetly two to three yards behind her were five security men. The prime minister was on her way to meet British actor-director Peter Ustinov, who was waiting with a television crew to conduct an hour long interview. He had been with her for two days as she campaigned through the state of Orissa in eastern India, and she had

enjoyed the actor's droll wit. 'The one thing I find utterly boring,' she had said, 'are second-rate journalists. But when I meet one who is smart and well informed, I find I give a much better interview.'"

Standing at attention more than halfway along the path were two khaki-uniformed security men wearing the traditional beards and turbans that identified them as Sikhs. One of them, Beant Singh, was one of her favourites: she had known him for ten years. The other was Satwant Singh, who had been with her for just five months. Gandhi put her hands together in a traditional Hindi greeting and said 'Namaste,' which means 'Greetings to you'. Beant Singh then drew his revolver and shot her three times in the abdomen. Satwant Singh followed that up by firing some 30 rounds from his Sten gun, of which seven penetrated her abdomen, three her chest and one her heart.

On the day before she was assassinated, she gave a speech at Orissa, where she said, 'I don't mind if my life goes in the service of the nation. If I die today every drop of my blood will invigorate India and keep a united India alive.'

Robert Kennedy, 1925–1968
'Don't lift me.'

A younger brother of President John F. Kennedy who served as one of his advisers during his presidency. From 1961 to 1964, he was the US Attorney General. He continued as Attorney General under President Lyndon B. Johnson for nine months. In September 1964, he resigned to seek the US Senate seat for New York, which he won in November. He then decided to aim for the presidency himself and won the California presidential primary in June 1968. He delivered his victory speech just after midnight on 5 June at the Ambassador Hotel in Los Angeles and as he was leaving he was shot by Sirhan Sirhan, a Palestinian Arab.

A well-informed report claimed that the man who was shaking his hand when he was shot was a man called Romero, who said that Kennedy asked, 'Is everybody safe, okay?' His wife Ethel was held back by the crowd, but eventually managed to reach him. He seemed to recognise her. As the medical team lifted Kennedy onto a stretcher, he was said to whisper, 'Don't lift me.' He lost consciousness shortly thereafter.

Objectively, it is very surprising that Kennedy was able to say anything. He had been shot three times and one bullet, fired at a range of about 1 inch, entered behind his right ear, dispersing fragments throughout his brain.

Huey P. Long, 1893–1935
'I wonder why he shot me?'

Fortieth Governor of Louisiana and a Democrat. On the day of his assassination he was at the State Capitol arguing a case which would lead to the dismissal of Judge Benjamin Henry Pavy. Pavy's son-in-law, Dr Carl Weiss, tried several times to talk to Long but was prevented from doing so by his bodyguards. At 9.20 p.m., Dr Weiss managed to get close to Long and fired a handgun at him at close range, hitting him in the stomach. Long's bodyguards returned fire, hitting Weiss many times and killing him. Long was rushed to the hospital but died two days later. His last recorded words were, 'I wonder why he shot me?'

Lord Melbourne, 1779–1848
'Die, my dear doctor. That's the last thing I shall do.'

William Lamb was born into an aristocratic family, although there was some doubt about his legitimacy. Marital controversy dogged him because his wife, Caroline, famously had an affair with Lord Byron. He was Home Secretary (1830–1834) and Prime Minister (1834 and 1835–1841), during which he provided very successful mentoring of the young and inexperienced Queen Victoria.

There was a famous court case in 1836 when the husband of his friend Caroline Norton tried to blackmail him. Melbourne refused to pay because he claimed he had done no wrong. Melbourne won the case, although he did stop seeing Mrs Norton. The last words attributed to him are frequently quoted also for Lord Palmerston: 'Die, my dear doctor. That's the last thing I shall do.'

Sir Thomas More, 1478–1535
'My neck is very short; take heed therefore thou strike not awry, for saving of thine honesty.'

More's father was a successful advocate and judge. A bright child, young Thomas served as a page to the Archbishop of Canterbury, who arranged for him to go to Oxford. He read Classics but stayed at university for only two years because his father insisted he should study law. In 1504 he was elected to Parliament but continued his legal duties and was under-sheriff of London from 1510. He proved to be an honest and effective public servant under Wolsey's protection, and became under-treasurer of the Exchequer. He succeeded Wolsey as Chancellor in 1529.

He was against the Reformation and resisted the theology of Martin Luther and William Tyndale, whose books he burned. More made himself very vulnerable when he refused to accept the king as Supreme Head of the Church of England. He also opposed the marriage to Anne Boleyn. He was tried for treason, convicted on dubious testimony and beheaded.

In William Roper's *The Life of Sir Thomas More*, he asserts that More's last words were to his executioner: 'Pluck up thy spirits, man, and be not afraid to do thine office; my neck is very short; take heed therefore thou strike not awry, for saving of thine honesty.'

Lord Palmerston, 1784–1865
'That's Article 98; now go on to the next.'

Henry John Temple served twice as Prime MInister. In early October 1865 Palmerston caught a chill and a violent fever. Worried about diplomatic treaties, his last words were reported as, 'That's Article 98; now go on to the next.'

Several internet sources claim that his final words were, 'Die, my dear doctor, that is the last thing I shall do,' words also attributed to Melbourne.

One myth reports that Queen Victoria was in the company of Palmerston and was the person who recorded his last remarks when he died. They were inspecting a regiment of the Guards and the queen complained that she could smell their sweat. Palmerston replied, 'Yes, Ma'am, it is known as *esprit de corps*.'

Spencer Perceval, 1762–1812
'Oh!'

The seventh son of the 2nd Earl Egmont, Spencer Perceval was born in Audley Square, London, on 1 November 1762. He holds the distinction of being the only British Prime Minister to have been assassinated. He was forty-nine and was shot at point-blank range in the House of Commons by John Bellingham, who had a grievance against the government because they had rejected his pleas for compensation after he was imprisoned in Russia. Perceval clutched his hand to his heart and said, 'Oh,' faintly before falling forward on his face, quite dead. Bellingham, who had no political motive, was hanged seven days later.

An online source suggests that he may have said, 'Murder,' or, 'Oh my God'. It also states that he did not die immediately, sustaining a light pulse while being moved to a room adjacent to the lobby of the House.

William Pitt the Elder, First Earl of Chatham, 1708–1778
'My Lords, any state is better than despair; if we must fall, let us fall like men.'

Pitt's family were wealthy but, as a younger son, he was not going to inherit the whole of the family fortune. Forced to choose a profession, he chose the Army and secured a commission as a cornet in the King's Regiment of Horse (which was later 1st the King's Dragoon Guards, and today is 1st the Queen's Dragoon Guards).

His military career was short because his brother secured two seats in the House of Commons and could only represent one. He passed the second to William.

He led Britain during the Seven Years' War and again with the official title of Lord Privy Seal between 1766 and 1768. He was a brilliant orator. Oddly he was out of power for most of his career, and became famous for his attacks on the government. His last appearance in the House of Lords was on 7 April 1778. He spoke for a considerable time, though with diminished vigour, against the motion being debated. After a response, he rose again to speak but collapsed. His last words before he died were, 'My Lords, any state is better than despair; if we must fall, let us fall like men.'

Another source suggests that his last words in the Commons were, 'If the Americans defend independence, they shall find me in their way,' and that his very last words (spoken to his son) were, 'Leave your dying father, and go to the defence of your country.'

William Pitt the Younger, 1759–1806
'I think I could eat one of Bellamy's veal pies.'

The second son of William Pitt the Elder, he became the youngest Prime Minister of Great Britain in 1783 at the age of twenty-four and was in office until 1801. He filled the office a second time for two years until his death in 1806. He was also the Chancellor of the Exchequer throughout his premiership.

Renowned for being thin and more fond of liquor than solids (he was known as a 'three bottle man', a reference to his heavy consumption of port), Pitt probably died from peptic ulceration of his stomach or duodenum. Reports said that his last words were, 'I think I could eat one of Bellamy's veal pies.'

Enoch Powell, 1912–1998
'I don't call that much of a lunch.'

The only child of a primary school headmaster, Enoch Powell had a fierce intellect. Before entering politics, he was a professor of Ancient Greek at the

"CLOSED! TRY THAT PLACE IN FLEET STREET. HE DOES A VERY NICE PIE. SWEENEY TODD..."

University of Sydney at the age of just twenty-five. He also flourished as a wartime soldier, becoming a brigadier at the age of thirty-two, and was one of just two men to rise from private to brigadier during the war (the other was Fitzroy Maclean). He was a Conservative Party Member of Parliament (1950–74) and Ulster Unionist Party (UUP) MP (1974–1987). In 1968 he made a controversial speech against immigration, now widely referred to as the 'Rivers of Blood' speech. Edward Heath promptly sacked him as Shadow Defence Secretary (1965–68). He had few friends in the establishment, possibly because few people could match or manage his brainpower.

He died aged eighty-five, at 4.30 a.m. on 8 February 1998 at the King Edward VII Hospital for Officers in the City of Westminster, London. On being told that he was being fed intravenously, he said, 'I don't call that much of a lunch.'

Adlai Stevenson, 1900–1965
'I feel faint.'

Although he was born in Los Angeles, Stevenson's family were long-term political heavies from Illinois. His grandfather was Vice President of the United States and his father, although not elected, was appointed as Secretary of State for Illinois. He himself became the Governor of Illinois and was

ocratic nominee for President in 1952 and 1956. He was defeated
Republican Eisenhower on both occasions and when he sought the
nation for a third time in 1960, he was beaten by John F. Kennedy.
Walking through Grosvenor Square in London with Marietta Tree he said,
feel faint,' and fell to the ground with such a crash that his companion
thought he had fractured his skull. He was dead anyway.

Leon Trotsky, 1879–1940
'I feel that this time they have succeeded.'

Russian revolutionary who founded the Politburo, served as People's
Commissar for Foreign Affairs and created and led the Red Army. Stalin
forced him into exile because of his opposition to his policies but, not
satisfied with the result, Stalin directed that he should be assassinated. His
final words were, 'I feel that this time they have succeeded.'

Emperor Vespasian, AD 9–79
'Vae, puto deus fio.'

Emperor from AD 69. His rise to the top came after Nero committed suicide,
which precipitated a year of civil war known as the Year of the Four Emperors.
Two, Galba and Otho, died in quick succession and Vespasian became Emperor
in April AD 69. On his deathbed he insisted that he should be helped to stand
because 'an emperor should die on his feet'. His last words were, 'Væ, puto deus
fio,' ('Woe is me. Methinks I am turning into a God') according to Suetonius.

Daniel Webster, 1782–1852
'I still live.'

Webster came from Salisbury, New Hampshire, one of ten children of a
farming family. He became a lawyer and indulged a growing interest in
politics. He was a good orator and determined nationalist, who became the
Senator for Massachusetts. His claim to fame is that he was on eleven US
postage stamps, something which even Presidents seldom achieve. He died
on 24 October 1852 at his home in Marshfield, Massachusetts, after falling
from his horse and suffering a crushing blow to the head.

The day before he died, his best friend, Peter Harvey, visited him. Webster
told Harvey, 'Be faithful, friend, I shall be dead tomorrow.' And he was! His
final words were said to be, 'I still live.'

Soldiers, Sailors, Airmen and Adventurers

Alexander the Great, 356–323 BC
'Κρατιστος.'

A brilliant soldier and campaigner, Alexander died in Babylon at the age of thirty-two, possibly as a result of poison. He had no heir and was asked on his deathbed who was to succeed him. He responded with one word, which some interpreted as 'Krateros', the name of one of his generals who was not among those present, and others chose to hear 'Κρατιστος. ('The strongest.')

General Ethan Allen, 1738–1789
'Waiting, are they? Well – let 'em wait.'

American Revolutionary general born in Connecticut. He was one of the founders of the state of Vermont, and is known for the capture of Fort Ticonderoga early in the American Revolutionary War. After the war he focused on local politics and his considerable estate. He was returning from visiting relatives at South Hero, Vermont, when he had an apoplectic fit and was unconscious by the time he reached home. It seems that a doctor attended him after he had the fit and sought to comfort him by saying, 'General, I fear the angels are waiting for you.' His response was, 'Waiting, are they? Waiting, are they? Well – let 'em wait.'

Mustafa Kemal Ataturk, 1881–1938
'Saat kaç?'

Outstanding soldier, Turkish hero of Gallipoli and first President of Turkey, from 1923 to 1938. Shortly before he fell into a coma on 6 November 1938 he asked, 'Saat kaç?' ('What time is it?')

Emperor Napoleon Bonaparte, 1769–1821
'France, armée, tête d'armée, Joséphine.'

An outstanding soldier, Napoleon proved his worth as a general and became Emperor of France from 1804 to 1815. He was defeated at the battle of Waterloo in 1815, and spent the final six years of his life in exile on the island of St Helena.

In February 1821, Napoleon's health began to fail rapidly and there have been suggestions that he was poisoned. His last words were, 'France, armée, tête d'armée, Joséphine.' ('France, army, head of the army, Joséphine.')

Gaius Julius Caesar, 100–44 BC
'καὶ σύ, τέκνον.'

Very effective Roman general and statesman, but not always the most popular of men. A conspiracy led to his murder by a number of assailants on the Ides of March. Interestingly, there is a report that only one of the many stab wounds on his body killed him. The dictator's last words are not known with certainty, and remain a contested subject among scholars and historians. Suetonius reported that others said Caesar's last words were the Greek phrase 'καὶ σύ, τέκνον' ('You too, child?'). But Suetonius himself affirmed that Caesar said nothing. Most people believe the version supplied by Shakespeare in his classic play, *Julius Caesar*: 'Et tu, Brute?'

Martha Jane Canary (better known as Calamity Jane), 1852–1903
'Bury me next to Bill.'

Frontierswoman and professional scout from Missouri, who claimed that she earned her nickname during a military campaign against American Indians. Many serious commentators reject that version of events. She also claimed that she had been the wife of Wild Bill Hickok and that her daughter was his. History records that at the time of his death, Hickok was newly married and not to Martha Jane Canary; in any event, Calamity Jane was working as a scout for the army when her child was born.

Her last words are said to have been, 'Bury me next to Bill.'

Giacomo Casanova, 1725–1798
'I have lived as a philosopher. I die as a Christian.'
Italian adventurer who was famed for his many elaborate affaires with women. He spent his last years in Bohemia as a librarian, where he also wrote the story of his life.

We cannot prove it, but most sources claim that his final words were, 'I have lived as a philosopher. I die as a Christian.'

Charlemagne, 747–814
'Lord, into Thy hands I commend my spirit.'
King of the Franks from 768, the King of Italy from 774, the first Holy Roman Emperor and the first emperor in western Europe since the collapse of the Roman Empire three centuries earlier. There is no credible contemporary record of his final words, although some sources claim he said, 'Lord, into Thy hands I commend my spirit.'

George S. Chavez, 1887–1910
'Higher, even higher.'
The words attributed to this brave young man are 'Higher, even higher' after crashing his Bleriot airplane on his trailblazing flight over the Alps. The reality must be different, because a contemporary account reported his successful flight over the Simplon Pass (6,600 feet) as part of a $14,000 Italian-sponsored contest in which thirteen aviators participated.

He flew a test flight which broke the altitude record by reaching 8,487 feet. On the day of the contest he was approaching the landing field but his aircraft failed. 'I saw the two wings of the monoplane suddenly flatten out and paste themselves against the fuselage,' a watcher said. 'Chavez was about a dozen meters up; he fell like a stone.' Four days later he died of massive internal injuries at the age of twenty-three.

Erskine Childers, 1870–1922
'Take a step forward, lads. It will be easier that way.'
Childers was born in London into an ecclesiastical family, although his mother's side owned land in County Wicklow. He attended Haileybury College and won an Exhibition to Trinity College, Cambridge. He and a friend enlisted in the Army to fight for the Empire in the Boer War but,

by the start of the First World War, his attitude to the Empire had turned through 180 degrees. Indeed, in 1914 he smuggled a shipment of arms to Irish Nationalists.

He is rightly remembered as the author of *The Riddle of the Sands*, which has never gone out of print.

In November 1922, Childers was arrested at home in Glendalough, County Wicklow, and was tried for the possession of a pistol. He was convicted and sentenced to death on 20 November. He appealed but the authorities moved too fast and he was executed on 24 November by firing squad at the Beggar's Bush Barracks in Dublin. Famously, he is credited with the statement, 'Take a step forward, lads. It will be easier that way.'

Christopher Columbus, 1451–1506
'Dios, en tus manos encomiendo mi espíritu.'

Italian explorer and navigator born in Genoa. Supported by the Catholic monarchs of Spain, he led four exploratory voyages across the Atlantic. On 20 May 1506, aged probably fifty-four, Columbus died in Valladolid, Spain. His last words were said to be, 'Dios, en tus manos encomiendo mi espíritu.' ('Lord, into Thy hands I commend my spirit.')

Captain James Cook, 1728–1779
'Take to the boats.'

A British explorer, navigator, cartographer, and captain in the Royal Navy. Cook led three voyages to the Pacific Ocean and claimed the first recorded European contact with the eastern coastline of Australia and the Hawaiian Islands. He also completed the first recorded circumnavigation of New Zealand.

Cook and his men enjoyed a month's stay on the island of Hawaii. Shortly after leaving, the foremast of the *Resolution* broke and the ships returned to Kealakekua Bay for repairs. The Hawaiians were not overjoyed. One of Cook's small boats was stolen and Cook's traditional response would have been to take hostages until the goods were returned. The Hawaiians resisted, and the naval team decided to withdraw. As he helped to launch the boats, Cook was knocked down and then stabbed to death.

According to Martin Terry in his article 'Remembering Cook,' his last words were probably, 'Take to the boats.'

Captain John Cooke, 1763–1805
'Let me lie a minute.'

An experienced and highly regarded officer of the Royal Navy who died in hand-to-hand combat with French forces during the Battle of Trafalgar in 1805. His ship HMS *Bellerophon* (nicknamed 'Billy Ruffian') was boarded by the French and Cooke was mortally wounded, probably by a sniper in the rigging of the French ship. His crew successfully drove off their opponents and ultimately forced the surrender of the French ship *Aigle*.

His last recorded words were, 'Let me lie a minute.'

Crowfoot, 1821–1890
'It is the little shadow which runs across the grass and loses itself in the sunset.'

He was a chief of the Blackfoot Nation tribe of Canada. Crowfoot died of tuberculosis at Blackfoot Crossing on 25 April 1890 and is credited with the following thoughtful final words.

'A little while and I will be gone from among you. Whither I cannot tell. From nowhere we came, into nowhere we go. What is life? It is a flash of a firefly in the night. It is the breath of a buffalo in the wintertime. It is the little shadow which runs across the grass and loses itself in the sunset.'

General Charles de Gaulle, 1890–1970
'Ça fait mal là.'

French general and statesman who led the Free French Forces during the Second World War. Later he was the first President of the Fifth Republic from 1959 to 1969.

On 9 November 1970, two weeks short of what would have been his eightieth birthday, he died suddenly, despite enjoying very robust health his entire life (except for a prostate operation a few years earlier). He had been watching the evening news on television and playing Solitaire. Around 7.40 p.m., he suddenly pointed to his neck and said, 'Ça fait mal là,' ('I feel a pain right here') before collapsing. His wife called the doctor and the local priest, but by time they arrived he had died from a ruptured blood vessel.

Jessica Dubroff, 1989–1996
'Do you hear the rain?'

A seven-year-old trainee pilot who attempted to become the youngest person to fly an aircraft across the United States. Tragically her flight instructor was flying the plane, a single-engine propeller aircraft, when it crashed after take-off from Cheyenne Regional Airport in Wyomingheyenne. Jessica, her father and the flight instructor died. It is not at all clear how her last words were recorded, but they are often published as, 'Do you hear the rain? Do you hear the rain?'

Amelia Earhart, 1897–1937
'We are running on line north and south.'

American pioneering aviator. Flying with Fred Noonan on an attempted flight around the World, they had completed 22,000 of their 29,000-mile planned trip. Their approach to Howland Island in the Pacific, some 1,700 nautical miles south-west of Hawaii, was unsuccessful. Their last radio message was, 'We are on the line 157–337. We will repeat this message. We will repeat this on 6210 kilocycles. Wait.' Shortly afterwards, she was heard on the same frequency (3105 kHz) saying, 'We are running on line north and south.'

In her last letter to her husband, George Putnam, she wrote, 'Please know that I am quite aware of the hazards. Women must try to do things as men have tried. When they fail, their failure must be but a challenge to others.'

Morgan Earp, 1851–1882
'I can't see a damned thing.'

The Earp brothers from Iowa were widely detested by the outlaws of the Wild West. Wyatt, Virgil and the younger Morgan worked in law enforcement in Arizona and all were involved in the gunfight at OK Corral. A survivor of that incident, a man called Clanton, managed to persuade the legal system to investigate the role of the Earps in what was branded murder. They were exonerated, but Clanton was determined to get revenge.

On Saturday 18 March 1882, Morgan Earp was the target of an assassination while he played a game of billiards. The gunman shot through a window facing onto a dark alley. The first bullet hit Earp and shattered his spine. A second bullet missed. His brothers tried to help him stand, but Morgan said, 'Don't, I can't stand it. This is the last game of pool I'll ever play.'

Wyatt and Morgan had promised each other that they would try to define any vision they had at the point of death. Wyatt reported that Morgan's last words were, 'I can't see a damned thing.'

General Ulysses Grant, 1822–1885
'I hope that nobody will be distressed on my account.'

The successful Unionist general who defeated the Confederate Army and ultimately became eighteenth President of the United States, from 1869 to 1877.

Grant died of throat cancer at the age of sixty-three in Mount McGregor. His last words were, 'I hope that nobody will be distressed on my account.' Some sources say that his final word was 'water'.

Nathan Hale, 1755–1776
'I only regret that I have but one life to lose for my country.'

Hale's family came from Connecticut. After completing his education at Yale, he joined the militia as a lieutenant. In 1776, during the Battle of Long Island, Hale volunteered for a mission in New York City, which was behind the British lines. He was captured and shot as a spy. He became something of a folk hero because of his last words, 'I only regret that I have but one life to lose for my country.'

Hannibal, 247–183 BC
'Liberemus diuturna cura populum Romanum, quando mortem senis expectare longum censent.'

Carthage was the principal city of an ambitious and militarily adventurous nation in what is modern-day Tunisia. Hannibal was a son of Hamilcar, a successful general of the First Punic War. But his son, Hannibal, proved to be one of the greatest military commanders in history.

The Romans eventually defeated the Carthaginians at the Battle of Zama, thereby bringing the Second Punic War to an end. Despite his defeat, Hannibal worked diligently at civil administration and became the chief magistrate. It took seven years, but Carthage became more prosperous and this alarmed the Romans. They wanted the man who had made it happen: Hannibal. He went into voluntary exile, but he realised that he was going to be hunted down. He was not prepared to fall into his enemies' hands so he took poison, which, it was said, he had long carried about with him in a ring. Before dying, he left behind a letter declaring, 'Liberemus diuturna cura populum Romanum, quando mortem senis expectare longum censent.' ('Let us ease the Roman people of their continual care, who think it long to await the death of an old man.')

John Henry 'Doc' Holliday, 1851–1887
'Damn. This is funny.'

American gambler, gunfighter and dentist, famous for his part in the gunfight at the OK Corral. He developed tuberculosis and his health deteriorated rapidly. He sought some relief from the curative waters at Glenwood Springs, Colorado, and stayed at the hotel, which has since become a more formal sanatorium. According to a nurse who was with him when he died, he looked at his bare feet and said, 'Damn. This is funny.'

Nobody would ever have imagined that he would die in bed with his boots off.

General Thomas 'Stonewall' Jackson, 1824–1863
'Let us cross over the river, and rest under the shade of the trees.'

Jackson's great-grandfather was an Ulsterman who was convicted of larceny in London, as was his wife, Elizabeth. They were both sentenced to be transported to America in 1749 and met on the good ship *Litchfield*. This is a timely reminder that England was shipping convicts out of the country long before they started to use Australia.

Young Thomas was born and brought up in Virginia and it was one of the tragedies of the Civil War that he and his sister, with whom he had been close, ardently embraced different sides. She was a Unionist, he a Confederate. He became one of the most well-known Confederate commanders after General Robert E. Lee. He was wounded in a friendly fire incident at the Battle of Chancellorsville.

Jackson died of pneumonia on 10 May 1863. On his deathbed he said, 'It is the Lord's Day; my wish is fulfilled. I have always desired to die on Sunday.' Seconds before he died, he cried out, 'Order A.P. Hill to prepare for action! Pass the infantry to the front rapidly! Tell Major Hawks.' There was a pause and then he said, 'Let us cross over the river, and rest under the shade of the trees.'

Ernst Kaltenbrunner, 1903–1946
'Deutschland, viel glück.'

The Austrian-born lawyer who took over the Reichssicherheitshauptamt after the assassination of Reinhard Heydrich, having joined the Nazi Party in 1932. He was tried at the International Military Tribunal at Nuremberg. He protested his innocence, claiming that his boss, Himmler, was responsible and that he was only obeying orders. He also said that he hardly knew Adolf Eichmann, although they had been boyhood friends in Linz. Found guilty on three counts of war crimes, he was hanged at Nuremberg on 16 October 1946. As the trap was sprung at 1.39 a.m., he said in a low voice, 'Deutschland, viel glück.' ('Germany, good luck.')

Genghis Khan, 1162–1227
'Hero. A real hero.'

It is almost impossible to tie down the facts of Genghis Khan's birth and upbringing. Suffice to note that his name was Temujin and he was a Mongolian. He became the Emperor of the Mongol Empire, which he created by uniting nomadic tribes of north east Asia. There is great confusion about his death, with some historians claiming that he fell off his horse; others say that he was wounded in battle. Marco Polo wrote that he died after the infection of an arrow wound. One source claims that he was stabbed by a princess who had been taken as booty. Frankly, no one knows. Legend has it that his final words were, 'Hero! A real hero.'

General Robert E. Lee, 1807–1870
'Tell Hill he must come up. Strike the tent.'

Lee was the son of a senior soldier who left his family. The young Robert hardly met his father and never spoke about his childhood. But the military influence had an effect and he carved out a career as a military engineer. He commanded the Confederate Army of Northern Virginia in the American Civil War, and was in command of the force which captured John Brown at Harper's Ferry in October 1859.

He had a stroke on 28 September 1870 and died two weeks later on 12 October in Lexington, Virginia, from pneumonia. According to one account, his last words were, 'Tell Hill he must come up. Strike the tent,' but this is debatable; Lee's stroke had resulted in aphasia, possibly rendering him unable to speak.

Captain Ernst Lehmann, 1886–1937
'It must have been an infernal machine.'

Lehmann was the most senior officer on the *Hindenberg*, although not its captain, when it caught fire at Lakehurst on 6 May 1937; he died the following day. Many sources claim that his final words were, 'Water, water,' but in fact he survived the disaster and escaped from the burning wreckage, saying to rescuers, 'I don't understand it.' During a deathbed conversation with Commander Charles Emery Rosendahl, he said, 'it must have been an infernal machine.'

General Grant, Marie Curie and Lenin all asked for water with their final breath.

Margaretha Geertruida Zelle McLeod (better known as Mata Hari), 1876–1917
'Tout est une illusion.'

A Dutch exotic dancer, courtesan and accused spy who was executed by firing squad in France, having been charged with espionage for Germany during the First World War. Allegedly her final words were, 'Tout est une illusion.' ('Everything is an illusion.')

Lieutenant Harry Harbord 'Breaker' Morant, 1864–1902
'Shoot straight, you bastards, and don't make a mess of it!'

Australian horseman, poet, soldier and convicted war criminal whose skill with horses earned him the nickname 'Breaker'. During the Second Boer War, Morant was accused of killing several Boer prisoners and a German missionary, Daniel Heese, who had been a witness to the shootings. He was court-martialled and executed for murder. As he waiting for the firing squad to get ready, he said to them, 'Shoot straight, you bastards, and don't make a mess of it!'

Hector Hugh Munro (Saki), 1870–1916
'Put that bloody cigarette out.'

The renowned author of amusing and often macabre stories, he was over-age when he enlisted to fight in the First World War. He refused a commission and joined as an ordinary trooper, rising to the rank of lance sergeant. In November 1916, when sheltering in a shell crater near Beaumont-Hamel during the Battle of the Ancre, he remonstrated with a soldier who was smoking. 'Put that bloody cigarette out,' he said, believing that the smoke would give away their position. Seconds later he was shot dead by a German sniper, who overheard the comment.

Ramón María Narváez, 1800–1868
'Yo no tengo que perdonar a mis enemigos. Los he tenido todo el tiro.'
1st Duke of Valencia. A professional soldier and statesman, he was made a field marshal in 1845. He served as prime minister on four separate occasions and was in office when he died in Madrid in April 1868. His last words were famously recorded on his deathbed. Asked if he forgave his enemies, he said, 'Yo no tengo que perdonar a mis enemigos. Los he tenido todo el tiro.' ('I do not have to forgive my enemies. I have had them all shot.')

Admiral Horatio Nelson, 1758–1805
'Thank God I have done my duty. Drink drink, fan fan, rub rub.'
The man who became a national hero for his naval exploits during the Napoleonic Wars and generally named as the victor of the Battle of Trafalgar in 1805. People tend to forget that Admiral Cuthbert Collingwood was the man who actually secured the victory after Nelson's death.

Nelson was mortally wounded by a bullet but took a long time to die. Many accounts of his death affirm that he said, 'Kiss me, Hardy,' or, 'Kismet, Hardy.' They were not his actual last words and Nelson's ship surgeon, Dr William Beatty, recorded that he said, 'Thank God I have done my duty. Drink drink, fan fan, rub rub.'

Captain Lawrence Oates, 1880–1912
'I am just going outside and may be some time.'

Oates was a complex character who served in the West Yorkshire Regiment and the 6th Inniskilling Dragoon Guards during the Boer War. In March 1901 he was shot in his thigh, which left it shattered and his left leg an inch shorter than his right leg. A doughty fighter, he was recommended for the Victoria Cross. In 1910, he joined Scott's famously tragic expedition to the South Pole.

Waking on the morning of 16 March 1912, Oates recognised that the expedition was nearing its end. He felt the need to sacrifice himself in order to give the others a chance of survival. Scott wrote that Oates said to them, 'I am just going outside and may be some time.' He walked out of the tent into a blizzard and -40 °C.

Joan of Arc, 1412–1431
'Jesus, Jesus, Jesus.'

Nicknamed 'The Maid of Orléans' (La Pucelle d'Orléans), she is a folk heroine of France and a Roman Catholic saint. From peasant stock, she was clearly an extraordinary woman because there is no doubting that she led the French army to several important victories during the Hundred Years War. This led to the coronation of Charles VII of France. She was captured and effectively sold to the English. She was tried by the pro-English Bishop of Beauvais Pierre Cauchon for 'insubordination and heterodoxy'. Inevitably, she was convicted and burned at the stake. She was just nineteen years old.

Twenty-five years after her execution, Pope Callixtus III authorised a court to investigate her actions and pronounced her innocent. She was declared a martyr and was beatified in 1909 and canonised in 1920.

It is said that her final words were, 'Jesus, Jesus, Jesus,' as she was consumed by flames.

Sir Walter Raleigh, 1544–1618
'Strike, man, strike!'

English aristocrat and explorer who introduced tobacco to England. Raleigh was a great favourite of Queen Elizabeth but fell from grace by secretly marrying one of her ladies-in-waiting. The queen found out a year after the event and was enraged. She imprisoned them both in the Tower of London from June to September 1592. Once restored to the queen's goodwill, his career prospered and from 1600 to 1603 he was Governor of Jersey.

The queen died in 1603 and Raleigh was arrested at Exeter Inn, Ashburton, Devon, and imprisoned in the Tower of London on 19 July 1603. On 17 November, Raleigh was tried in Winchester Castle for treason. He denied the charges but was found guilty and sentenced to death. The king spared his life, but he remained in the Tower until 1616. He was released in order to conduct a second expedition to Venezuela in search of El Dorado. On Raleigh's return to England, the Spanish ambassador successfully demanded that King James reinstate Raleigh's death sentence. Raleigh was brought to London from Plymouth.

Raleigh was beheaded at the Palace of Westminster on 29 October 1618. 'Let us dispatch,' he said to his executioner. 'At this hour my ague comes upon me. I would not have my enemies think I quaked from fear.' He was shown the axe that was going to be used and said, 'This is a sharp medicine, but it is a physician for all diseases and miseries.' According to many biographers – for instance, Raleigh Trevelyan in *Sir Walter Raleigh* (2002) – Raleigh's final words were, 'Strike, man, strike!'

Other sources claim that his final words were, 'So the heart be right, it is no matter which way the head lieth.' There are variations on this version ('What does it matter how the head lies, so the heart be right?') A further source asserts that he said, 'I have a long journey to take, and must bid the company farewell.'

Manfred von Richthofen, 1892–1918
'Kaputt.'

A German fighter pilot with the Imperial German Army Air Service during the First World War. He is considered the top ace of that war, being officially credited with eighty air-combat victories. Known as the Red Baron, he was a hero in Germany and a respected foe among the Allies. He was shot down and killed near Amiens on 21 April 1918.

Many sources claim that his last known words were, 'Wozu die Eile? Haben Sie Angst, ich werde nicht wiederkommen?' ('What's the hurry? Are you afraid I won't come back?') Eyewitnesses at his death included Sergeant Ted Smout of the Australian Medical Corps, who reported that Richthofen's last word was 'Kaputt' ('bust').

Captain Robert F. Scott, 1868–1912
'For God's sake, look after our people.'

A Royal Navy officer and explorer who led two expeditions to the Antarctic. On his second expedition he led a party of five, which reached the South Pole on 17 January 1912. They discovered that they had been beaten by Roald Amundsen's Norwegian expedition. On their return journey, Scott and his four comrades all died. The final words in his diary were, 'Last entry. For God's sake, look after our people.'

General John Sedgwick, 1813–1864
'They could not hit a bull at this dis–'

He was the highest-ranking Union soldier killed during the American Civil War. His last words were spoken at the Battle of Spotsylvania Courthouse, where he was riding along the line of his own troops, who encouraged him to be careful. He responded, 'Why, man, they couldn't hit an elephant at this dis–'

(Bill Bryson says it was the Battle of Fredericksburg, and affirms that the words were, 'I tell you, men, they could not hit a bull at this dis–')

Private Smith, 5th Canadian Black Watch, ?–1945
'I'll see you in twenty minutes, sir.'

During Operation Veritable between the Maas and the Rhine rivers in the village of Gennep, Captain Donald Beales established his company headquarters in a house in the town. He sent his runner, Private Smith, with a message to another part of his company. As he moved down the road, Private Smith shouted, 'I'll see you in twenty minutes, sir.' The next minute, Beales was killed. Rather spookily, Smith was killed twenty minutes later.

William Wallace, 1270–1305
'Freedom.'

Scottish landowner who became one of the key leaders in the Scottish Wars of Independence. He was one of the successful commanders of the army that beat the British at the Battle of Stirling Bridge in 1297 but was beaten comprehensively at the Battle of Falkirk in 1305. He was captured near Glasgow and on the orders of King Edward I he was hanged, drawn and quartered for high treason.

His last words were not recorded but, according to the film *Braveheart*, his final statement was, 'Freedom.'

Arthur Wellesley, Duke of Wellington, 1769–1852
'Yes. If you please.'

Woken at 0630 by his valet, Kendall. Half an hour later a maid heard him 'making a great noise' and Kendall rushed to his room to see what was wrong. The Duke asked for his doctor. 'I wish to speak to him.' Dr Hulke was having breakfast at home in Deal and rushed immediately to the Castle. It seemed there was no great cause for concern but half an hour after the doctor left, Kendall asked the Duke if he would like some tea. 'Yes, if you please,' he replied. Those were his last words because he was then gripped by a series of fits, lapsed into unconsciousness and died at 3.25 p.m.

Wellington: A Journey Through My Family, Lady Jane Wellesley, 2008; with permission.

Lieutenant John Scott Youll, VC, 1897–1918
'It's all right, Cowling, we got them stone cold.'

A colliery electrician from Thornley, Durham, who was an officer in the Royal Engineers attached to the 11th Battalion Northumberland Fusiliers when he won his VC on 15 June 1918.

Sadly he was to die a fortnight before the Armistice and, according to Michael Ashcroft's book *Victoria Cross Heroes*, he was still only twenty-one when he was struck by a shell and killed in the major assault on the Piave River on 27 October 1918. He had just said, 'It's all right, Cowling, we got them stone cold.'

US Presidents

President John Adams, 1735–1826
'Thomas Jefferson survives.'

Second President of the United States (1797–1801). He was the first President to reside in the 'President's Mansion', which later became known as the White House. He narrowly lost re-election in 1800 to Thomas Jefferson.

On 4 July 1826, the fiftieth anniversary of the adoption of the Declaration of Independence, Adams died at his home in Quincy. Told that it was the Fourth, he answered, 'It is a great day. It is a good day.' He then said, 'Thomas Jefferson survives.' (Actually, Jefferson had died earlier that same day.) Some, including Brewer's *Dictionary of Phrase and Fable*, say that his last words were, 'Independence forever.'

President John Quincy Adams, 1767–1848
'This is the last of earth. I am content.'

The son of President John Adams, he became the sixth President of the United States (1825–1829). He is the only President to have been elected to the House of Representatives after his presidency. Representing Massachusetts, he served for seventeen years with, some say, greater distinction than during his presidency.

On 21 February 1848, the House of Representatives was discussing how to honour US Army officers who served in the Mexican–American War. Adams firmly opposed this idea, so when the rest of the house erupted into 'ayes', he cried out, 'No!' and collapsed, having had a cerebral haemorrhage. Two days later, on 23 February, he died with his wife and son at his side. His last words were, 'This is the last of earth. I am content.'

President James Buchanan, 1791–1868
'Oh Lord God Almighty, as thou wilt.'

Fifteenth President of the United States, from 1857 to 1861. The only President to be a lifelong bachelor after a failed courtship with Anne Caroline Coleman. She broke off their engagement, then committed suicide. Buchanan never paid attention to women thereafter.

He died of respiratory failure at his home in Pennsylvania and is alleged to have uttered the final words, 'Whatever the result may be, I shall carry to my grave the consciousness that at least I meant well for my country. Oh Lord God Almighty, as thou wilt.'

President Grover Cleveland, 1837–1908
'I have tried so hard to do right.'

He served as the twenty-second and twenty-fourth President of the United States. Cleveland is the only President to serve two non-consecutive terms (1885–1889 and 1893–1897) and therefore is the only individual to be counted twice in the numbering of the presidents.

In 1893 he was diagnosed with a malignant cancer in the mouth. He decided to have his surgery in secrecy in order to avoid further panic that might affect the financial depression. Under the cover of a holiday cruise, surgeons operated aboard the yacht *Oneida* as it sailed off Long Island. Unbelievably, the story hardly reached the press and when it did, the surgeons managed to deflect suspicion. Cleveland survived for many years after the removal of the tumour and died eventually of a heart attack. His final words are commonly accepted to have been, 'I have tried so hard to do right.'

President Calvin Coolidge, 1872–1933
'Good morning, Robert.'

Thirtieth President of the United States, from 1923 to 1929. A rather serious, even dull man, he was dubbed 'Silent Cal'. He died suddenly at his home of a coronary thrombosis. There are two versions of his final words. Shortly before his death, he confided to an old friend, 'I feel I no longer fit in with these times.' Other sources claim that he said, 'Good morning, Robert,' to the carpenter who was working on his home, the Beeches.

President Dwight D. Eisenhower, 1890–1969
'I want to go. God, take me.'

Thirty-fourth President of the United States, from 1953 to 1961. During the Second World War he was a five-star general commanding the Allied efforts in North Africa and the invasion of Europe. He served as the first Supreme Commander of the Allied Forces in Europe.

He died of congestive heart failure on 28 March 1969, in the Walter Reed Army Hospital, Washington. His last words were reported to be, 'I've always loved my wife, my children, and my grandchildren, and I've always loved my country. I want to go. God, take me.'

President Millard Fillmore, 1800–1874
'The nourishment is palatable.'

Thirteenth President of the United States, from 1850 to 1853. He came to the presidency by virtue of being Vice President to Zachary Taylor, who died in office. History does not hold him in high regard and he is probably one of the least well known of US Presidents.

He died at 11.10 p.m. on 8 March 1874, having had a stroke. His last words were alleged to be, upon being fed some soup, 'The nourishment is palatable.'

President James Garfield, 1831–1881
'Oh Swaim, there is a pain here. Swaim, can't you stop this? Oh, oh, Swaim!'

Twentieth President of the United States, who served for just 200 days in 1881. He was shot by the assassin Charles Guiteau. Thanks to the invention of Alexander Graham Bell, he was the first President to speak on the telephone. Bell was at the other end, 13 miles away. He said, 'Please speak a little more slowly.' His final words were, 'Oh Swaim, there is a pain here. Swaim, can't you stop this? Oh, oh, Swaim!' David Swaim was his Chief of Staff.

President Warren G. Harding, 1865–1923
'That's good. Go on. Read some more.'

Twenty-ninth President of the United States, from 1921 to 1923. During the last week of his life he was unwell, possibly with pneumonia, although some commentators think that he had a severe bout of food poisoning. He and his wife had travelled to San Fransisco from Oregon and were staying at the Palace Hotel. He was given digitalis and caffeine that helped relieve his heart condition and sleeplessness. The President's health appeared to improve, so his doctors went to dinner. Unexpectedly, during the evening, he shuddered and died abruptly in the middle of conversation with his wife. She was reading him an article from the newspaper and he said, 'That's good. Go on. Read some more,' then died.

President Benjamin Harrison, 1833–1901
'Are the doctors here? Doctor, my lungs!'

Twenty-third President of the United States, from 1899 to 1893. Grandson of William Henry Harrison, the ninth President and the only President ever to come from Indiana. Six states were admitted to the Union during his presidency: North and South Dakota, Montana, Washington, Idaho and Wyoming.

He died of pneumonia at home, saying, 'Are the doctors here? Doctor, my lungs!'

President William Henry Harrison, 1773–1841
'Sir, I wish you to understand the true principles of the government. I wish them carried out. I ask nothing more.'

Ninth President of the United States in 1841, an American military officer and politician. He was the first President to die in office and the last President to be born before the United States Declaration of Independence. Harrison served the shortest term of any American president: 4 March–4 April 1841, 30 days, 12 hours, and 30 minutes.

His last words were to his doctor, but assumed to be directed at John Tyler. 'Sir, I wish you to understand the true principles of the government. I wish them carried out. I ask nothing more.'

President Rutherford B. Hayes, 1822–1893
'I know that I am going where Lucy is.'

Ninteenth President of the United States, from 1877 to 1881. When he was elected, he pledged not to stand for a second term.

He died at home after a heart attack. His final words were, 'I know that I am going where Lucy is.' He was referring to his much-loved wife who had died four years earlier.

President Herbert Hoover, 1874–1964
'Levi Strauss was one of my best friends.'

Thirty-first President of the United States, from 1929 to 1933. He died from massive internal bleeding. When told that Admiral Strauss had come to pay him a visit, Hoover said, 'Levi Strauss was one of my best friends,' then died.

President Andrew Jackson, 1767–1845
'Oh, do not cry – be good children and we will all meet in Heaven.'

Seventh US President, from 1829 to 1837. He was a tough and aggressive man, which earned him the nickname 'Old Hickory.' He killed several people in duels and was a wealthy slaveholder.

On 30 January 1835, Jackson was leaving the Capitol when Richard Lawrence, an unemployed workman from England, aimed a pistol at Jackson. It misfired so Lawrence pulled out a second pistol, which also misfired. Lawrence was restrained by the famous Davy Crockett and Jackson is said to have attacked Lawrence with his cane.

Andrew Jackson died from tuberculosis and heart failure. His final words were said to be, 'Oh, do not cry – be good children and we will all meet in Heaven.'

President Thomas Jefferson, 1743–1826
'Is it the fourth yet?'

An American founding father and the principal author of the Declaration of Independence (1776). He was the third President of the United States, from 1801 to 1809.

By May 1826 Jefferson's health was desperately frail. During the last hours of his life he was surrounded by family and friends, all awaiting the expected departure. He was at ease and was ready to die. Close to the end, he called the rest of his family and friends around his bedside and pronounced, 'I have done for my country, and for all mankind, all that I could do, and I now resign my soul, without fear, to my God – my daughter to my country.' He then nodded off and later awoke, asking, 'Is it the fourth yet?' His doctor replied, 'It soon will be'. It was the fiftieth anniversary of the Declaration of Independence and he died a few hours before John Adams, whose last words were, 'Independence forever,' and, 'Thomas Jefferson survives.'

President Andrew Johnson, 1808–1875
'My right side is paralysed. I need no doctor. I can overcome my own troubles.'

Johnson was Vice President to Abraham Lincoln, so moved into the top job when his boss was assassinated in 1865. He was in office until 1869.

He was staying with his daughter Mary when he had a stroke. He refused to let her send for a doctor until the next day. Two doctors were sent for from Elizabethton. He seemed to respond to their treatment, but suffered another stroke on the evening of July 30, and died early the following morning at the age of sixty-six.

Allegedly his final words were to his granddaughter (some say it was his daughter). 'My right side is paralysed. I need no doctor. I can overcome my own troubles.'

President Lyndon B. Johnson, 1908–1973
'Send Mike immediately.'

Thirty-sixth President of the United States, thrust into office by the assassination of his predecessor, John F. Kennedy. He was President from 1963 to 1969.

His health was poor in retirement, not least because he had put on too much weight, smoked heavily and had angina. He survived several heart attacks but on the afternoon of 22 January 1973 he had a massive heart attack which killed him. He managed to pick up a telephone and said to the Secret Service agent who answered, 'Send Mike immediately.' The agent and others ran to Johnson's bedroom and found him on the bed, still holding the telephone but dead.

President John F. Kennedy, 1917–1963
'No, you certainly can't.'

'Jack' Kennedy was elected as the thirty-fifth President of the United States, taking office in 1961. As the golden son of a political dynasty, his election as President had some sense of inevitability. Kennedy is the only Catholic President, and is the only one to have won a Pulitzer Prize. Events during his presidency included the Bay of Pigs Invasion, the Cuban Missile Crisis, the building of the Berlin Wall, the Space Race, the African–American Civil Rights Movement, and early stages of the Vietnam War.

The trip to Texas, during which he was assassinated by Lee Harvey Oswald, was seen by some as courting danger. He was there to smooth political tensions between liberals and conservatives in his own Democratic Party. Rather spookily, on arrival in Dallas, he said, 'If someone is going to kill me, they will kill me,' but these were not his final words, which some have claimed to be, 'That's obvious.'

The Connellys were riding in the car with the President. Nellie Connelly, wife of Governor John Connelly, commented, 'You certainly can't say that the people of Dallas haven't given you a nice welcome, Mr President.'

He replied 'No, you certainly can't.' He was assassinated seconds later.

President Abraham Lincoln, 1809–1865
'It doesn't really matter.'

Sixteenth President of the United States, serving from March 1861 until his assassination in April 1865. Lincoln led the United States through the Civil War. He preserved the Union, abolished slavery, strengthened the national government and modernised the economy.

On 14 April 1865, Lincoln and his wife attended a play, *Our American Cousin*, at Ford's Theatre. The bodyguard left the theatre during the interval to join the coachman for a drink next door. The President sat unaware in his state box in the balcony. Booth spotted his opportunity and managed to get within inches of the President, then shot him at point-blank range.

There was a report that the Lincolns were discussing his desire to see Jerusalem. Another source claims that his final words were, 'It doesn't really matter,' said in response to his wife's admonition not to hold her hand at the theatre, because people might see them.

President James Madison, 1751–1836
'Nothing more than a change of mind, my dear. I always talk better lying down.'

Fourth President of the United States, who served from 1809 to 1817. As Jefferson's Secretary of State, he supervised the Louisiana Purchase, which doubled the nation's size. He died on his estate, Montpelier, in Virginia. Some sources say that his final words were, 'Nothing more than a change of mind, my dear. I always talk better lying down.'

This was in response to a niece, who asked, 'What is the matter, Uncle James?'

President William McKinley, 1843–1901
'God's will be done, not ours.'

Twenty-fifth President of the United States, serving from 4 March 1897 until his assassination in September 1901. McKinley led the nation to victory in the Spanish–American War.

During a delayed visit to the Pan American Exposition in Buffalo, New York, on 6 September 1901, McKinley was shot twice in the stomach by an anarchist, Leon Czolgosz. One bullet was deflected by a button, causing no damage. The second was lodged in his gut and the surgeon who attended him had no experience of stomach operations. The bullet was not found, so the wound was tidied up and left. The President seemed to prosper but gangrene set in and he died in the early hours of 14 September. McKinley realised his condition and said, 'It is useless, gentlemen. I think we ought to have prayer.' Relatives and friends gathered around his bed as his wife wept that she wanted to go with him. 'We are all going, we are all going,' he replied. 'God's will be done, not ours.' By some accounts, those were his final words; he may also have sung part of his favourite hymn, 'Nearer My God to Thee'.

President James Monroe, 1758–1831
'I regret that I should leave this world without again beholding him.'

Fifth President of the United States, who served from 1817 to 1825. Monroe was the final president who was a founding father of the United States. Curiously, he was also the third of them to die on Independence Day. He is probably most remembered for articulating the Monroe Doctrine.

He died in New York from heart failure and tuberculosis; his reported last words were, 'I regret that I should leave this world without again beholding him.' He was referring to James Madison.

President Richard M. Nixon, 1913–1994
'Help!'

Thirty-seventh President of the United States, from 1969 to 1974. He is the only President to resign the office, which he was obliged to do after the Watergate Scandal. Nixon had a severe stroke on 18 April 1994. He was taken to Cornell Medical Center in Manhattan, initially alert but unable to speak or to move his right arm or leg. Damage to the brain caused swelling (cerebral edema), and Nixon slipped into a deep coma. He died at 9.08 p.m. on 22 April 1994, with his daughters at his bedside. He was eighty-one years old. Some reports say that his last word was, 'Help!'

President James K. Polk, 1795–1849
'I love you, Sarah. For all eternity, I love you.'

Eleventh President of the United States, from 1845 to 1849. Many consider him one of the greatest presidents for his ability to set an agenda and achieve all of it. The White House destroyed his health. A vigorous and enthusiastic man when he entered office, he was exhausted four years later. He died at his new home in Nashville, Tennessee, on 15 June 1849, a mere 103 days after leaving office. His sincere devotion to his wife was enshrined in his final words: 'I love you, Sarah. For all eternity, I love you.' She survived him by a further forty years.

President Ronald Reagan, 1911–2004
Not recorded

Fortieth President of the United States, from 1981 to 1989, who started his working life as an actor. He is the only President to have been divorced. In

1994, he announced that he had been diagnosed with Alzheimer's disease. He died ten years later at the age of ninety-three.

It is ironic that the man often called 'the Great Communicator' was unable to converse at his death. His daughter reported that he used his eyes to bid farewell to his family. His burial site is inscribed with the words he delivered at the opening of the Ronald Reagan Presidential Library: 'I know in my heart that man is good, that what is right will always eventually triumph and that there is purpose and worth to each and every life.'

President Franklin D. Roosevelt, 1882–1945
'I have a terrific pain in the back of my head.'

Thirty-second President of the United States, from 1933 to 1945. He led the United States through economic depression and world war. He was a dominant leader of the Democratic Party and the only American president elected to more than two terms.

In August 1921, while the Roosevelts were on holiday in Canada, Roosevelt contracted polio, which resulted in permanent paralysis from the waist down.

During the afternoon of 12 April 1945, he said, 'I have a terrific pain in the back of my head.' He then collapsed and never spoke again. He died of a cerebral haemorrhage.

President Theodore Roosevelt, 1858–1919
'Put out the light.'

Twenty-sixth President of the United States. He was an energetic 'man's man' who was admired for his many interests and activities. He also served in public office at every level of administration. He was forty-two years old when sworn in as President of the United States in 1901, making him the youngest president ever. Roosevelt was also the first of only three sitting presidents to have won the Nobel Peace Prize. The teddy bear is named after him, despite his dislike of being called 'Teddy'.

While campaigning in Milwaukee, Wisconsin, on 14 October 1912, a saloon keeper shot him. The bullet went through his steel glasses case and a thick folded copy of a speech in his pocket. Most of the force had dissipated before it reached his body. Roosevelt correctly concluded that, since he was not coughing blood, the bullet had not completely penetrated the chest wall to his lung, and so refused to go to the hospital. Instead, he delivered his scheduled speech with blood seeping into his shirt. He spoke for ninety minutes. His opening comments to the gathered crowd were, 'Ladies and gentlemen, I don't know whether you fully understand that I have just been shot; but it takes more than that to kill a bull moose.'

On 16 January 1919, Roosevelt died in his sleep at Oyster Bay of a heart attack; his last words, 'Put out the light,' were the request to his second wife, Edith, that they finish for the day.

President Zachary Taylor, 1784–1850
'I regret nothing but I am sorry to leave my friends.'

Twelfth President of the United States, from 1849 to 1850, and successful military leader during the Mexican–American War. Many people believe that Taylor was poisoned by pro-slavery Southerners. In the late 1980s, a former professor at University of Florida managed to persuade the family and the authorities to order an exhumation to resolve the continuing rumours. No evidence of poisoning was found and it was agreed that he had probably died of cholera morbus. Any potential for recovery was profoundly undermined by his doctors, who treated him with ipecac, calomel, opium and quinine. They bled and blistered him too.

His final words were, 'I am about to die. I expect the summons very soon. I have tried to discharge all my duties faithfully. I regret nothing but I am sorry to leave my friends.'

President John Tyler, 1790–1862
'I am going. Perhaps it is best.'

Tenth President of the United States, who served from 1841 to 1845. He was the first to succeed to the office on the death of the incumbent, succeeding William Henry Harrison. He was also the first person to serve as President without ever being elected. He holds one further record, which is that he fathered more children than any other President (eight by his first wife and seven by the second). Interestingly, his first daughter, Mary, died in 1847 and his last daughter, Pearl, died one hundred years later in 1947.

He suffered poor health throughout his life and was bedridden for his final week. The doctor was called and just after midnight Tyler took a sip of brandy and told his doctor, 'I am going. Perhaps it is best.'

President Martin Van Buren, 1782–1862
'There is but one reliance.'

Eighth President of the United States, from 1837 to 1841. English was not his first language because he was brought up speaking Dutch. He died of bronchial asthma and heart failure at his Lindenwald estate in Kinderhook at 2.00 a.m. on 24 July 1862 and the only record of his final words claims that he said, 'There is but one reliance.'

President George Washington, 1732–1799
''Tis well.'

The first US President, who served from 1789 to 1797. Many different versions of his final words exist. The most popular is, 'I die hard but am not afraid to go. Let me go quietly. I cannot last long. It is well.' Another is, 'I am just going. Have me decently buried and do not let my body be put into the vault in less than three days after I am dead.'

But his biography differs. As with later presidents, the doctors probably hastened his end with their treatment, which including bleeding and laxatives. In the modern world, he would almost certainly have survived.

His final words came after he invited his personal manservant, Christopher Sheels, to sit down because he was so fatigued after standing by the great man's bed for many hours. The last words were, ''Tis well,' as he felt his own wrist, then expired.

President Woodrow Wilson, 1856–1924
'I am ready.'

Twenty-eighth President of the United States who was in office from 1913 to 1921. In 1919 he had a serious stroke, which paralysed his left side and left him blind in his left eye. He spent weeks in bed and was confined to a wheelchair. This was one of the most serious cases of presidential disability in American history and was later cited as an argument for the 25th Amendment, which deals with succession to the presidency. The full extent of his disability was kept from the public until after his death from another stroke on 3 February 1924. His last words were, 'I am ready.'

Royalty

Prince Albert of Saxe-Coburg, the Prince Consort, 1819–1861
'I have such sweet thoughts.'

The husband of Queen Victoria. He found difficulty in adapting to his position as consort. He had no formal duties, but over time adopted many public issues and took on the duty of running the queen's household, estates and office. He was the moving force in the organisation of the Great Exhibition of 1851.

The contemporary diagnosis of his death was typhoid fever, but Albert was ill for at least two years before his death, which suggests that a chronic disease, such as Crohn's disease, renal failure or cancer was the cause of death. Two versions of his final words have been published: 'I have such sweet thoughts,' and, 'I have had wealth, rank and power; but if these were all I had, how wretched I should be!'

Tsar Alexander II (Romanov), 1818–1881
'Помогите!'

The Emperor of Russia from 2 March 1855 until his assassination in 1881. He was known as Alexander the Liberator for securing the emancipation of serfs in 1861.

On 13 March 1881, Alexander was the victim of a plot to kill him in Saint Petersburg.

For many years he went to the Mikhailovsky Manège for the military roll call on Sunday. He travelled in a closed carriage accompanied by Cossacks and guards. The carriage was followed by two sleighs carrying the chief of police and the chief of the emperor's guards. The route never varied.

The assassin threw his bomb under the horses' hooves. The explosion killed and injured people nearby and one of the guards, but the emperor emerged shaken but unhurt. The assassin was captured almost immediately. However, a second young plotter threw something at the emperor's feet. He was alleged to have shouted, 'It is too early to thank God.' The explosion was deafening. The Tsar moaned, 'Помогите!' ('Help!') His legs were shattered, his stomach was ripped open and his face badly damaged. Blood gushed out of him.

Later it was learned there was a third bomber in the crowd, ready to act if the first two attempts failed.

Popular mythology has it that his final words were, 'I am sweeping through the gates, washed in the blood of the Lamb,' but it is most unlikely that he said much after the initial cry for help.

Queen Anne Boleyn, 1501–1536
'To Jesus Christ I commend my soul; Lord Jesus receive my soul.'

Second wife of Henry VIII and Queen of England 1533–1536. It is possible down the years of history to feel considerable sympathy for Anne. She resisted Henry's advances, but he was an immovable force of nature who would always get his own way. True, she will have been tempted by the thought of becoming queen, but she didn't really understand the vicious circles of the court.

On 7 September 1533, she gave birth to the future Elizabeth I of England, whose gender disappointed Henry. He fondly imagined that a boy would appear eventually, but three miscarriages left Henry bored with Anne. He started courting Jane Seymour. Thomas Cromwell was given the task of finding a way for Henry to get rid of one for the other, and he patched together a hollow case of adultery and incest with a range of men, including Anne's own brother. Tried for high treason by a court of peers, which included her uncle and her first fiancé, she was sentenced to death and was executed at the Tower of London on 19 May 1536.

On the day of her execution, she said to her jailer, 'The executioner is, I believe, an expert, and my neck is very slender. Oh God, have pity on my soul, oh God, have pity on my soul.'

On the scaffold she gave a short speech to the crowd, then she knelt upright, praying. 'To Jesus Christ I commend my soul; Lord Jesus receive my soul.' According to the late Eric W. Ives, the executioner Rombaud was so taken by Anne that he was shaken. Rombaud found it so difficult to proceed that to distract her and for her to position her head correctly, he shouted, 'Where is my sword?' just before killing her.

King Charles 1, 1600–1649
'Stay for the sign.'

In Simon Schama's extensive programme about English history, he says that King Charles I's last words were, 'A subject and a sovereign are clearly a different thing.' But this brief ending is refuted by the contemporary report of the Whitehall newspaper whose reporter was beside the scaffold. It shows that the final words were, 'Stay for the sign.' This sign was the king's instruction to his executioner to strike when the king extended his hands.

King Charles II, 1630–1685
'I am sorry, gentlemen, for being such a time a-dying'.

Cromwell died in 1658, but it was not until 29 May 1660 that the thirty-year-old King Charles II arrived back in England. He was crowned at Westminster Abbey on 23 April 1661.

Charles had an apoplectic fit on the morning of 2 February 1685, and died four days later. Inevitably there was suspicion of poison in the minds of many, including one of the royal doctors. Modern medical analysis suggests that actually it was a kidney dysfunction. On his deathbed Charles asked his brother, James, to look after his mistresses. 'Be well to Portsmouth, and let not poor Nelly starve.' He also said to his courtiers, 'I am sorry, gentlemen, for being such a time a-dying.'

King Charles V of France, 1338–1380
'Ay, Jesus.'

Of the House of Valois, he was King of France from 1364 until his death. His reign represented a high point for France in the Hundred Years War, with his armies recovering much of the territory ceded to the English under the Treaty of Bretigny.

He died on 16 September 1380 and was succeeded by his twelve-year-old son, Charles VI. Some sources say that his final words were 'Ay, Jesus'.

King Charles VIII, 1470–1498
'J'espère ne plus jamais commettre un péché mortel, ni même véniel, si je peux l'aider.'

King of France from 1483 until his death. He died in 1498 after accidentally striking his head on the lintel of a door as he was en route to watch a game of Jeu de Paume (real tennis). His last words were said to be, 'J'espère ne plus jamais commettre un péché mortel, ni même véniel, si je peux l'aider.'

('I hope never again to commit a mortal sin, nor even a venial one, if I can help it.') In all honesty, this version of events is most unlikely because he went into a deep coma when he hit his head and never recovered consciousness.

King Charles IX, 1550–1574
'Priez Dieu pour moi. Adieu.'

A Valois King of France from 1560 until his early death. During the French Wars of Religion, which involved a series of engagements between Catholics and Protestants, it is said that between 2 and 4 million people died. Charles did try to reconcile his people, but also allowed the murder of Huguenot leaders in Paris.

He was not a well man and he privately acknowledged his part in the death of the Huguenots. Words that are generally attributed to him are: 'Qu'est-ce sang versé! Que meurtres! Quel mal conseil, j'ai suivi! O mon Dieu, pardonne-moi ... Je suis perdu! Je suis perdu!' ('What blood shed! What murders! What evil council I have followed! O my God, forgive me ... I am lost! I am lost!')

But the fact is those words were uttered long before he died and it was on his last day, 30 May 1574, that Charles called for Henry of Navarre, embraced him, and said, 'Mon frère, vous perdez un bon ami. Si j'avais cru tout ce qu'on m'a dit, tu ne serais pas en vie. Mais j'ai toujours aimé vous ... J'ai confiance en toi seul pour m'occuper de ma femme et mon fils. Priez Dieu pour moi. Adieu.' ('Brother, you are losing a good friend. Had I believed all that I was told, you would not be alive. But I always loved you ... I trust you alone to look after my wife and son. Pray God for me. Farewell.')

Princess Diana, 1961–1997
'Leave me alone.'

On 31 August 1997, Diana, the divorced wife of Charles, Prince of Wales, was fatally injured in a car crash in the Pont de l'Alma road tunnel in Paris, which also caused the deaths of Dodi Fayed and the driver, Henri Paul.

She is reported to have said to her rescuers, 'Leave me alone.' Others reported that she said, 'My God. What's happened?'

King Edward III, 1312–1377
'Jesu, have pity.'

King of England, 1327–1377. Edward's health deteriorated sharply in his last eight months of life. He probably had a stroke on 21 June, when he suddenly lost the power of speech. He lay in his bed, unable to do or say anything. The only people with him were his mistress, Alice, and a priest. Eventually Alice removed all of his rings from his fingers and left the room. The priest remained, praying beside his bed, exhorting the king to repent of his sins. Perhaps the priest's report of the king's last words had more to do with optimism than reality: 'Jesu, have pity.'

King Edward VI, 1537–1553
'I am faint; Lord have mercy upon me, and take my spirit.'

King of England, 1547–1543. Always a sickly child, he died at the age of fifteen. Most commentators believe the cause was tuberculosis, although there were rumours of poison (a common theme for royalty throughout history).

Edward died on 6 July 1553. According to John Foxe's legendary account of his death, his last words were, 'I am faint; Lord have mercy upon me, and take my spirit.'

King Edward VII, 1841–1910
'I am very glad.'

Son of Queen Victoria, he was King of the United Kingdom and the British Dominions and Emperor of India from 22 January 1901 until his death in 1910.

Edward smoked constantly. Towards the end of his life he suffered increasingly from bronchitis and was staying at Biarritz in March 1910 when he collapsed. He remained there to convalesce, despite political tensions in England. On 27 April he returned to England. Days later he had several heart attacks, but refused to go to bed, saying, 'No, I shall not give in; I shall go on; I shall work to the end.' The Prince of Wales (shortly to be King George V) told him that his horse, Witch of the Air, had won at Kempton Park that afternoon. The king replied, 'I am very glad,' which proved to be his final words.

Empress Elisabeth of Austria, 1837–1898
'Nein, was ist mit mir geschehen?'

Wife of Franz Joseph I, and therefore both Empress of Austria and Queen of Hungary. She also held the titles of Queen of Bohemia and Croatia. Family and close friends called her Sisi.

On 10 September 1898, Elisabeth and her lady-in-waiting Countess Irma Sztáray de Sztára et Nagymihály walked from their hotel to catch the steamship for Montreux. They were walking along the promenade when a young Italian approached them. According to Sztáray, the assassin seemed to stumble and made a movement with his hand as if he wanted to maintain his balance. In reality, he had stabbed Elisabeth with a sharpened needle file. The empress collapsed but was helped to her feet and escorted on board the steamship. Elisabeth revived and Sztáray asked her if she was in pain. She replied, 'Nein, was ist mit mir geschehen?' ('No, what has happened to me?') She then lost consciousness and died.

As an aside, it must be said that the empress had little physical strength to carry her through the experience. She is said to have died with a 12-inch waist, which was the product of her extraordinary eating routine. Her staple diet was pressed duck, from which she drank the juices.

Queen Elizabeth I, 1533–1603
Not recorded

The 'Virgin Queen' who became Queen of England at the age of twenty-five, a mere four years after being incarcerated in the Tower of London by her half-sister, Mary, on suspicion of being involved in Wyatt's rebellion.

She enjoyed good health for most of her life but in the autumn of 1602 several of her close friends died. She plunged into a deep depression and in March 1603 she fell sick and remained in a 'settled and unremovable melancholy'. She died on 24 March 1603 at Richmond Palace, between two and three in the morning. Many sources claim that her final words were, 'All my possessions for a moment of time,' but they are probably apocryphal. She is thought to have lost the power of speech some time before she died, so no one managed to capture the right words when they were uttered.

Archduke Franz Ferdinand of Austria-Hungary, 1863–1914
'Es ist gar nichts – es ist gar nichts ... '

Heir presumptive to the Austro-Hungarian throne. Nobody could have predicted that his death would be the catalyst for war. There were plenty of other reasons for the central European powers to sabre rattle, but the Archduke's assassination in Sarajevo was the spark that lit the fire.

Immediately after being shot he said to his aide, Count Harrach, 'Es ist gar nichts – es ist gar nichts ... ' ('It is nothing – it is nothing ... '). He then lapsed into unconsciousness and died.

King Frederick V, 1723–1766

'Det er en stor trøst for mig i min sidste time, at jeg har aldrig forsætligt fornærmet nogen, og at der ikke er en dråbe blod på mine hænder.'

King of Denmark and Norway, 1746–1766. He was an alcoholic whose reign was saved by very able ministers. His last words were reportedly, 'Det er en stor trøst for mig i min sidste time, at jeg har aldrig forsætligt fornærmet nogen, og at der ikke er en dråbe blod på mine hænder.' ('It is a great consolation to me in my last hour that I have never wilfully offended anyone and that there is not a drop of blood on my hands.')

King George IV, 1762–1830

'Good God, what is this? My boy, this is death. They have deceived me.'

King of England, 1820–1830. This was a man who enjoyed his food and drink immeasurably. He was obese and derided by the people whenever he appeared in public. He died at about half-past three in the morning of 26 June 1830 at Windsor Castle; he reportedly called out to his page, 'Good God, what is this? My boy, this is death. They have deceived me.' This is attributed also to King William IV.

King George V, 1865–1936
'God damn you!'

King of the United Kingdom who came to the throne on the death of his father, King Edward VII, on 6 May 1910. He became the first monarch of the House of Windsor in 1917 when he abandoned the name 'House of Saxe-Coburg and Gotha' as a result of anti-German public sentiment.

Popular mythology has it that his final words were, 'Bugger Bognor,' after his physician suggested that he take a break at his palace in Bognor. The reality is different.

On the evening of 15 January 1936, George said that he had a cold and went to his bedroom. He became gradually weaker, drifting in and out of consciousness. According to his secretary, he said, 'How is the Empire?' This does sound like the carefully considered memorial of a loyal secretary, who reported that his answer was, 'All is well, sir, with the Empire.' The King gave him a smile and relapsed once more into unconsciousness.

On 20 January Lord Dawson of Penn, his doctor, issued a bulletin: 'The king's life is moving peacefully towards its close.' Dawson's private diary, which became public in 1986, said that the king's final words were, 'God damn you!' and were addressed to his nurse when she gave him a sedative on the night of 20 January.

King Henry V, 1386–1422
'You lie, you lie. My portion is with the Lord Jesus.'

King of England from 1413 until his death. His greatest military success was victory at the Battle of Agincourt. There were months of diplomacy with Charles VI of France, finally creating the Treaty of Troyes, which recognised Henry V as regent and heir apparent to the French throne. He then married Charles's daughter. Henry died of dysentery at the Palace of Vincennes, near Paris. He was a devout Christian and his last words were to an imagined antagonist. 'You lie, you lie. My portion is with the Lord Jesus.'

King Henry VIII, 1491–1547
'All is lost. Monks, monks, monks!'

The much-married King of England is alleged to have said on his death in 1547, 'All is lost. Monks, monks, monks!' Many commentators believe he was syphilitic, but it is far more likely that he died of Type 2 Diabetes.

King Louis XIV, 1638–1715
'Pourquoi pleurez-vous. Avez-vous pensez que j'étais immortel?'

Known as Louis the Great and 'the Sun King', he reigned from 1643 until his death, a reign of seventy-two years and 110 days. One source attributes a lengthy speech to the dauphin as his final words, urging him to be a force for good, with the final sentence being, 'Lighten your people's burden as soon as possible, and do what I have had the misfortune not to do myself.'

Other sources say that his last words to his attendants were, 'Pourquoi pleurez-vous. Saviez-vous que j'étais immortel?' ('Why do you weep? Did you think I was immortal?') Yet another attribution is, 'Je m'en vais, mais l'Etat demeurera toujours.' ('I depart, but the State remains forever.')

King Louis XVI, 1754–1793
'Je prie Dieu que le sang que vous allez verser ne peut jamais être visité sur la France.'

King of France from 1774 until 1792, when he was deposed. He was executed by guillotine on 21 January 1793, not as a king, but as citizen Louis Capet.

He was the only King of France ever to be executed. His death brought to an end more than a thousand years of continuous French monarchy.

He addressed his executioners, 'Je meurs innocent de tous les crimes prévus à ma charge, je pardonne à ceux qui ont causé ma mort, et je prie Dieu que le sang que vous allez verser ne peut jamais être visité sur la France.' ('I die innocent of all the crimes laid to my charge; I pardon those who have occasioned my death; and I pray to God that the blood you are going to shed may never be visited on France.')

King Louis XVIII, 1755–1824
'Un Roi doit mourir debout.'

Known as 'the Desired', he was a monarch of the House of Bourbon who ruled as King of France and Navarre from 1814 to 1824, except for a period in 1815 known as the Hundred Days. His health began to fail in the spring of 1824. He was obese and had gout and gangrene, both dry and wet, in his legs and spine. His final words were, 'Un Roi doit mourir debout.' ('A king should die standing.')

Queen Louise of Prussia, 1776–1810
'Ich bin eine Königin, aber ich habe nicht die Macht, meine Arme zu bewegen.'

The wife of King Frederick William III, with whom she enjoyed a happy marriage and produced nine children. She was greatly loved in Prussia, and when she died it was said that the king had lost his best minister. On 19 July 1810, while visiting her father in Strelitz, the queen died in her husband's arms from an unidentified illness. Her reported final words were, 'Ich bin eine Königin, aber ich habe nicht die Macht, meine Arme zu bewegen,' ('I am a queen, but I have not the power to move my arms.')

Queen Marie Antoinette, 1755–1793
'Pardonnez-moi, monsieur. Je ne l'ai pas fait exprès.'

Baptised Maria Antonia Josepha Johanna (or Maria Antonia Josephina Johanna) and born an Archduchess of Austria, she was Dauphine of France from 1770 to 1774 and Queen of France and Navarre from 1774 to 1792. She was the fifteenth and penultimate child of Holy Roman Emperor Francis I and Empress Maria Theresa.

The monarchy was abolished on 21 September 1792. The royal family was imprisoned and months after the death of her husband Marie Antoinette was tried and sentenced to death. She was executed by guillotine on 16 October 1793. As she mounted the scaffold, she inadvertently stood on her executioner's foot and said, 'Pardonnez-moi, monsieur. Je ne l'ai pas fait exprès.' ('Pardon me, monsieur, I did not mean to do it.')

Another source claims she said, 'Farewell, my children, forever. I go to your father.'

Mary, Queen of Scots, 1542–1587.
'In manus vestras, Dómine.'

She was the only surviving legitimate child of King James V of Scotland and was six days old when her father died. She spent her childhood in France and in 1558 married François, the Dauphin of France. He ascended the French throne as King François II in 1559. Widowed in 1560, Mary returned to Scotland, arriving in Leith on 19 August 1561. Four years later, she married her first cousin, Henry Stuart, Lord Darnley, but their union was unhappy. In February 1567, his residence was destroyed by an explosion, and Darnley was found murdered in the garden.

The 4th Earl of Bothwell was suspected of having organised Darnley's death but he was exonerated in April 1567, and promptly married Mary. They were not a popular or successful team and she was forced to abdicate in favour of James, her one-year-old son by Darnley. She made an unsuccessful attempt to regain the throne, which left her with little option but to seek the

"HAVE YOU HAD AN ACCIDENT AT WORK? THEN GUILLOTINE LAWYERS FOR YOU..."

protection of her cousin, Queen Elizabeth I of England. She was in a difficult position. She had tried to claim the throne of England as her own, and many English Catholics favoured her cause. Perceiving her as a threat, Elizabeth had her confined in a number of castles and manor houses in the interior of England. After eighteen and a half years in custody, Mary was found guilty of plotting to assassinate Elizabeth, and was executed.

Mary's execution was curious. Frail and in need of physical help, as she put her head onto the block, she said, 'Into your hands, O Lord,' three times, then again in Latin, 'In manus vestras, Dómine.' It took two goes with the axe to remove her head. When the executioner lifted up her head, he found that he had a wig in his hand and the actual head was still on the scaffold. No one had known that she had lost her hair. Then her body appeared to move. Underneath her skirt was her Skye terrier.

Emperor Maximilian of Mexico, 1832–1867
'Viva México! Viva la Independencia.'

He was proclaimed Emperor of Mexico on 10 April 1864. He was formerly the Archduke Maximilian of Austria. His reign was not a success and by 1866 he was being urged to abdicate. Rebellion followed. He was captured, court-martialled and sentenced to death.

He died in front of a firing squad on 11 June 1867, saying, 'Yo perdono a todos. Rezo para que todo el mundo también me puede perdonar, y mi sangre, que está a punto de arrojar traerá la paz a México. Viva México! Viva la Independencia.' ('I forgive everybody. I pray that everybody may also forgive me, and my blood which is about to be shed will bring peace to Mexico. Long live Mexico! Long Live Independence!')

Tsar Nicholas II of Russia, 1868–1918
'Что? Что?'

In March 1917 the Tsar was forced to abdicate. The Kerensky Government was unsure what to do with the Romanov family and a half-thought plan of exile in England was rejected by King George V on the advice of his ministers. Initially, therefore, they were sent to Tobolsk in the Urals, but after the Bolsheviks seized power, life became harsher. On 30 April 1918 they moved to Yekaterinburg, where they were held in the two-story Ipatiev House, which ominously became referred to as the 'house of special purpose'.

There are several accounts of what happened and historians have never agreed. Yurovsky, the chief executioner, gave an account that on 17 July 1918, the royal family was woken around 2.00 a.m., told to dress and led down into a half-basement room. The pretext for this move was the family's safety.

A firing squad was waiting in an adjoining room. When the family arrived in the basement, the former empress asked for chairs. Yurovsky ordered that two chairs be brought in (another source says that three chairs were brought in), and when the empress and the tsar were seated, the executioners appeared. Yurovsky announced that they had been condemned to death. A stunned Nicholas asked, 'Что? Что?' ('What? What?') and turned toward his family. Yurovsky quickly repeated the order and shot the former emperor dead.

Queen Victoria, 1819–1901
'Bertie.'
Queen of the United Kingdom of Great Britain and Ireland from 20 June 1837. From 1 May 1876, she was also Empress of India. Her reign marked a great expansion of the British Empire.

She was distraught after the early death of her husband, Albert, on 14 December 1861 and for a prolonged period retired from public life.

Her relationship with her children was fractious. She sought to control her children and not all of them would comply. Her eldest son was very much his own man, so there is a certain piquancy in her final word, 'Bertie,' uttered in astonishment when he entered the room. Her son and successor King Edward VII, and her eldest grandson, Emperor Wilhelm II of Germany, were at her deathbed. Indeed, some say that Kaiser Wilhelm was holding her in his arms when she died. Her favourite pet Pomeranian, Turri, was laid upon her deathbed as a last request.

King William I (the Conqueror), 1028–1087
'So I chastised a great multitude of men and women with the lash of starvation and, alas, was the cruel murderer of many thousands, both young and old, of this fair people.'
William the Bastard, Duke of Normandy, conqueror of Harold at the Battle of Hastings and ruler of England from 1066 to 1087. According to an account written in *Historia Ecclesiastica* by Orderic Vitalis, sixty-five years after his death, he said,

'I treated the native inhabitants of the kingdom with unreasonable severity, cruelly oppressed high and low, unjustly disinherited many, and caused the death of thousands by starvation and war, especially in Yorkshire. In mad fury I descended on the English of the north like a raging lion, and ordered that their homes and crops with all their equipment and furnishings should be burnt at once and their great flocks and herds of sheep and cattle slaughtered everywhere. So I chastised a great multitude of men and women with the lash of starvation and, alas, was the cruel murderer of many thousands, both young and old, of this fair people.'

King William I of Prussia, 1797–1888
'Ich habe keine Zeit, müde zu sein.'

He was King of Prussia (1861–1888) and the first German Emperor (1871–1888). Working with his favoured Minister, Otto von Bismarck, William achieved the unification of Germany and the establishment of the German Empire.

Despite many assassination attempts on his life, William was a popular king and died a natural death in Berlin. His final words were, 'Ich habe keine Zeit, müde zu sein.' ('I haven't got time to be tired.')

King William IV, 1765–1837
'It is death, my boy. They have deceived me.'

King of the United Kingdom and of Hanover from 26 June 1830 until his death. Although there is no tangible evidence for it, many sources claim that his final words were, 'Wally, what is this? It is death, my boy: they have deceived me.' This is attributed also to King George IV.

King William I, Prince of Orange, 1533–1584
'Mon Dieu, ayez pitié de mon âme; mon Dieu, ayez pitié de ce pauvre peuple.'

Also known as William the Silent. Phillip II of Spain offered a reward of 25,000 crowns for the assassination of William, a task which was taken on by Balthasar Gerhardts, who made an appointment to see the prince. William was dining in his home in Delft with a guest when Gerhardts arrived. William left the room and his guest heard him being shot. His dying words were, 'Mon Dieu, ayez pitié de mon âme; mon Dieu, ayez pitié de ce pauvre peuple.' ('My God, have pity on my soul; my God, have pity on this poor people.')

Clerics

Pope Alexander VI, 1431–1503
'Mi sento molto male.'

Born Roderic Llançol i de Borja. Head of the Catholic Church from 11 August 1492 until 1503. His name, Borgia, became a byword for libertine practices and nepotism. To counter that, two of Alexander's successors, Sixtus V and Urban VIII, described him as one of the most outstanding popes since St Peter.

One source claims that his final words were, 'Va bene, va bene, arrivo. Aspettate un momento.' ('Ok, ok, I'll come. Just give it a moment.') In fact this is most unlikely because he was desperately ill and confined to his bed. The report of his final hours states that he gave his confession to Bishop Gamboa of Carignola, who then read Mass to him. It was attended by five cardinals, Serra, Juan and Francesco Borgia, Casanova and Loris. The Pope told them that he felt very bad – 'Mi sento molto male.' At the hour of vespers, after Gamboa had given him Extreme Unction, he died.

Pope John Paul I, 1912–1978
'Ci vediamo domani, se Dio vuole.'

Born Albino Luciani, he was head of the Catholic Church from 26 August to 28 September 1978. He died of a heart attack and was found sitting up in bed with working papers in his hand. His final words, to one of his house staff, were, 'Ci vediamo domani, se Dio vuole.' ('I will see you tomorrow, if God wills it.')

Pope John Paul II, 1920–2005
'Pozwólcie mi odejść do domu Ojca.'

Born Karol Wojtyla, a Pole born in Wadowice, he became the first non-Italian pope since Pope Adrian VI in 1523. He survived two assassination attempts, in 1981 and 1982, although he was severely wounded by the gunman in the first attempt. On Saturday 2 April 2005, at about 15.30 CEST, John Paul II spoke his final words, 'Pozwólcie mi odejść do domu Ojca,' ('Allow me to depart to the house of the Father') to his aides, and fell into a coma about four hours later.

Archbishop Thomas Becket, 1120–1170
'Semper valete.'

Archbishop of Canterbury. On Tuesday 29 December 1170 Becket's assassins, Reginald fitz Urse, Hugh de Morville, William de Tracy and Richard Brito, faced Becket in Canterbury Cathedral. Clearly understanding what was about to happen, the archbishop said, 'I am ready to die for my Lord, so that in my blood the Church may obtain peace and liberty. But I forbid you in the name of God Almighty and on pain of excommunication to harm any of my men, whether clerk or lay.'

Shortly after Christmas 1170 Becket wrote a note – his final written words – to William of Norwich, one of his most stalwart supporters, who had expressed the desire to see the archbishop again before he died. Becket's note read, 'Semper valete.' ('Farewell for ever.')

Venerable Bede, 673–735
'It is well. You have said the truth. It is indeed.'

English monk at the Northumbrian monastery of Saint Peter at Monkwearmouth and of its companion monastery, Saint Paul's, in modern Jarrow. An author and scholar, he wrote *Historia ecclesiastica gentis Anglorum* (*The Ecclesiastical History of the English People*). He died after dictating the final sentence of his translation of the Gospel of St John. His scribe reported that the sentence had been written. 'It is well,' he said. 'You have said the truth. It is indeed.'

Saint Boniface, ?–754
'It is another thing to die than people have imagined.'

Apostle of the Germans, born Winfrid, Wynfrith or Wynfryth in the kingdom of Wessex, probably at Crediton. He was a missionary and the first Archbishop of Mainz. He was killed with fifty-two others at Dokkum in Frisia by armed locals who thought that they might find treasure. After the slaughter, they were dismayed to discover no more than religious manuscripts.

One story has it that he died by the sword, and another that the assailants poured boiling lead into his mouth. The legend is that his last words were, 'It is another thing to die than people have imagined.' On the other hand, the Bonifacian vitae record that Boniface persuaded his armed comrades to lay down their arms, saying, 'Cease fighting. Lay down your arms, for we are told in Scripture not to render evil for good but to overcome evil by good.'

Cesar Borgia, 1475–1507
'E ora, purtroppo. Sono a morire, anche se del tutto impreparati.'

Italian nobleman, politician and cardinal. He was the son of Pope Alexander VI and his long-term mistress Vannozza dei Cattanei. He was the brother of Lucrezia Borgia, Giovanni Borgia (Juan), Duke of Gandia, and Gioffre Borgia (Jofré in Catalan), Prince of Squillace. After the death of his brother in 1498 he became the first person to resign his post as a cardinal. His father gave him land from the Papal States, but after his father's death, although he was a very able soldier, he was unable to retain power. He was killed in the early morning of 12 March 1507 while fighting just outside of the city of Viana, Spain.

The traditional record of his final words is, 'Avevo previsto nel corso della mia vita, per tutto tranne la morte. E ora, purtroppo. Sono a morire, anche se del tutto impreparati.' ('I had provided, in the course of my life, for everything except death. And now, alas, I am to die, though entirely unprepared.')

Dominique Bouhours, 1628–1702
'Je suis sur le point – ou je vais mourir. Soit l'expression est correcte.'

French Jesuit priest, essayist and neoclassical critic. He was born and died in Paris. His *Doutes sur la langue française proposés aux Messieurs le l'Académie française* was called 'the most important and best organised of his numerous commentaries on the literary language of his time'. There is something attractive about his last words, which were, 'I am about to – or I am going to die. Either expression is correct.'

Jesus Christ, *c.* 7–2 BC – AD 30–36
'Eli Eli lama sabachthani?'

Most modern historians accept that Jesus existed as a Jewish teacher from Galilee who was crucified in Jerusalem on the order of Pontius Pilate. His final words are enshrined in the Gospels.

In Mark 15:34, he said, 'Eli Eli lama sabachthani?' which is, 'My God, my God, why have you forsaken me?'

Thomas Cranmer, 1489–1556
'Lord Jesus, receive my spirit ... I see the heavens open and Jesus standing at the right hand of God.'

A leader of the English Reformation and Archbishop of Canterbury during the reigns of Henry VIII, Edward VI and, for a short time, Mary I. After the death of King Edward VI, Cranmer supported Lady Jane Grey's cause, so Mary's accession to the throne placed Cranmer in opposition to his new monarch. He was imprisoned, tried for treason and found guilty. After two years in prison, he was burned at the stake, creating some dismay when he departed from an agreed text by denouncing the Pope. As the flames licked around his body, he put out his right hand, which had signed his recantations, to be burned first, saying, 'That unworthy hand,' then, finally, 'Lord Jesus, receive my spirit ... I see the heavens open and Jesus standing at the right hand of God.'

Jan Huss, 1369–1415
'O sancta simplicitas!

Born in Bohemia, he was a Czech philosopher, priest and martyr. He was burned at the stake for heresy against the doctrine of the Catholic Church. As the flames licked around the pyre, he noticed a peasant adding a faggot and said, 'O sancta simplicitas!' ('O holy simplicity!')

Malcolm Little, better known as Malcolm X, 1925–1965
'Let's cool it, brothers.'

Also known as El-Hajj Malik El-Shabazz, he was an African American Muslim minister and human rights activist. To his admirers, he was a courageous advocate for the rights of blacks. Detractors accused him of racism, black supremacy and violence.

On 21 February 1965, a disturbance broke out in the 400-person audience that Malcom X was going to address. A man yelled, 'Nigger! Get your hand outta my pocket!'

Malcolm X and his bodyguards moved to quiet the disturbance, with

Malcolm X saying, 'Let's cool it, brothers.' A man seated in the front row rushed forward and shot him once in the chest with a double-barrelled sawn-off shotgun. Two other men fired semi-automatic handguns, hitting Malcolm X several times. According to the autopsy report, Malcolm X's body had twenty-one gunshot wounds to his chest, left shoulder, and arms and legs.

Dwight L. Moody, 1837–1899
'Earth is receding, heaven is opening. This is my coronation day.'

Famous American Evangelist preacher and founder of the Moody Church and Moody Bible Institute. He preached his last sermon in November 1899 in Kansas City, Missouri. He felt ill and returned home by train to Northfield, Massachusetts. In the months before he died he added some 30 pounds to his already ample frame. Although his illness was never diagnosed, commentators believed that he experienced congestive heart failure. On his deathbed he is reported to have said, 'Can this be death? Why it is better than living! Earth is receding, heaven is opening. This is my coronation day.'

Charles Haddon Spurgeon, 1834–1892
'This is my coronation day. I can see the chariots, I'm ready to board.'

British Baptist preacher who is known as the 'Prince of Preachers'. He was a prolific author and many of his sermons were transcribed as he spoke and were translated into many languages during his lifetime. He died at Menton in France and it is said that his final words were, 'I can hear them coming! Don't you hear them? This is my coronation day. I can see the chariots, I'm ready to board.'

Saint Stephen, ?–AD 34
'Look! I can see the heavens opening and the Son of Man standing at the right hand of God.'

A follower of Jesus, a Greek-speaking Hellenistic Jew who is traditionally seen as the first martyr of Christianity. From Acts 7:56 Stephen is about to be stoned to death by an angry crowd of Jews for proclaiming Jesus to be the promised Messiah. Suddenly he has a rapturous vision in which he sees Jesus in heaven, wrapped in the glory of God. His final words were, 'Look! I can see the heavens opening and the Son of Man standing at the right hand of God.'

Anonymous, Impersonal

Alex the African Grey Parrot

Used in comparative psychology research at Brandeis University. Dr Irene Pepperberg put Alex the parrot in his cage for the night in September 2007. The parrot said, 'You be good. See you tomorrow. I love you.' Sadly, he was lying dead on the cage floor in the morning.

Anonymous words found scratched on a wall in Pompeii

'Nihil in rerum natura maneat semper.' ('Nothing in the world can endure forever.')

Crew of Challenger, 28 January 1986

Mission Control: 'Challenger, go at throttle up.'

Challenger: 'Roger, go at throttle up.'

Static – Pause –

Mission Control: 'Flight controllers here are looking very carefully at the situation. Obviously a major malfunction.'

Mission STS-51-L disintegrated over the Atlantic Ocean, off the coast of central Florida. The disaster occurred after an O-ring seal in its right solid rocket booster failed at lift-off. The external tank failed completely and aerodynamic forces promptly broke up the orbiter.

Message found in a bottle purporting to have been launched by William Graham

The bottle was found on a Hebridean island in 1861 and the message read, 'On board the *Pacific* from Liverpool to N.Y. – Confusion on board – icebergs around us on every side. I know I cannot escape. I write the cause of our loss that friends may not live in suspense. The finder will please get it published.'

The SS *Pacific* was a wooden-hulled steamer built in 1849 for transatlantic service with the American Collins Line. She set a new transatlantic speed record in her first year of service, but disappeared without trace on a voyage from Liverpool to New York. The details of the *Pacific*'s fate remained a mystery for years. In 1991, wreckage located in the Irish Sea off the coast of Wales was identified without corroboration as the SS *Pacific*.

The name *Pacific* was not a great success for the shipping world. Another SS *Pacific* was a 876-ton sidewheel steamer built in 1851; it sank in 1875 as a result of a collision southwest of Cape Flattery, Washington. The *Pacific* had an estimated 275 passengers and crew aboard when it sank. Only two survived.

Hindenberg Airship

On 6 May 1937, 'Over Forked River. Course Lakenhurst,' was the last wireless message from the doomed airship.

Titanic, 1912

The final signal was 'V.....V...'

Titanic crew member, 1912

As he gave Minnie Coutts his lifejacket, he said, 'There, if the boat goes down, you will remember me.'

Literature and Films

Abel Magwitch (from *Great Expectations* by Charles Dickens)
'That's best of all.'

Magwitch is the escaped convict made good, who secretly funds the upbringing of Pip, the central character. Magwitch makes the mistake of returning to England incognito and is recaptured, having drowned his old rival, Compeyson. His re-engagement with Pip is not immediately successful, but eventually Pip regards Magwitch as a friend and frequently visits him in jail. On what proved to be his final visit, Pip held his hand and Magwitch said, 'And what's the best of all, you've been more comfortable along of me since I was under a dark cloud than when the sun shone. That's best of all.' He had spoken his last words, and, holding Pip's hand in his, passed away.

Miss Havisham (from *Great Expectations* by Charles Dickens)
'Take the pencil and write under my name, "I forgive her."'

A wealthy spinster who lives in her ruined mansion, looked after by her niece, Estella. She was left at the altar by Compeyson, who sought only to defraud her. Her life is dedicated to revenge, which she achieves by encouraging Estella to break the hearts of men as hers was broken by Compeyson. But she repents late in the novel when Estella leaves to marry Pip's rival, Bentley Drummle, and she realises that she has caused Pip's heart to be broken in the same manner as her own. Rather than achieving any kind of personal revenge, she has only caused more pain. Miss Havisham begs Pip for forgiveness.

After Pip leaves, Miss Havisham's dress catches on fire from her fireplace. Pip rushes back and saves her. She has suffered severe burns to the front of her torso. The last words she speaks in the novel are to Pip, referring both to Estella and a note she, Miss Havisham, has given him: 'Take the pencil and write under my name, "I forgive her."'

Marcus Aurelius, Roman Emperor 161–180 (from 2000 film *Gladiator*, directed by Ridley Scott)
'Commodus, your faults as a son are my failure as a father.'

He is widely seen as one of the 'good' emperors of Rome and in the film is seen to prefer Maximus, the general (and ultimately gladiator), as his preferred successor, although historically Marcus gave the succession to his son Commodus, whom he had named Caesar in 166 and made co-emperor in 177. This decision, which put an end to the series of adoptive emperors, was highly criticizsd by later historians since Commodus was a political and military outsider, as well as an extreme egotist with neurotic problems.

But in the film, Marcus tells his son that Maximus will be his heir. His final words in the film are, 'Commodus, your faults as a son are my failure as a father,' before Commodus asphyxiates him.

Commodus, Roman Emperor 177–192 (also from *Gladiator*)
'Give me your sword.'

Third-rate Emperor, who murdered his own father and sought to fatally injure the gladiator, Maximus, deciding to fight Maximus in the ring. Even though he is dying, Maximus is too good for him and, during a sword duel, Commodus finds himself without a weapon. His final words were addressed to the captain of his guard, Quintus: 'Give me your sword. ' Quintus declined to hand over a weapon.

Kolva (from *City of Thieves* by David Benioff)
'It's not the way I pictured it.'

This was after he had been shot by fellow Russians at the conclusion of an expedition to find a dozen eggs.

Boromir, Captain of the White City (from *The Lord of the Rings* by J. R. R. Tolkien)
'Go to Minas Tirith and save my people! I have failed.'

This famous death scene has been adapted many times. The original, taken from the novel after Boromir is fatally wounded by a party of orcs, is, 'Farewell, Aragorn! Go to Minas Tirith and save my people! I have failed.'

In the 1978 film, *The Lord of the Rings*, these words become, 'The halflings – orcs took them. I think they are not dead.'

And in the 2001 film, *The Fellowship of the Ring*, he says to Aragorn, 'I would have followed you, my brother – my captain – my king.'

King Arthur (from *Le Morte d'Arthur* by Sir Thomas Malory)
'And if thou hear never more of me, pray for my soul.'

King Arthur knows that he is dying and instructs Sir Bedivere to throw his sword into the lake. Bedivere pretends to do so twice, but fails to deceive the king. On the third occasion, Excalibur is caught by a mysterious arm rising out of the lake. Once Arthur has been laid into a barge among ladies dressed in black, it becomes apparent that he will not return; Sir Bedivere cries out in distress.

"'Comfort thyself,' said the king, "and do as well as thou mayst, for in me is no trust for to trust in; for I will into the vale of Avilion to heal me of my grievous wound: and if thou hear never more of me, pray for my soul.'"